LYDIA BRIGHT

Live, Laugh, Love, Always, Lydia

TOWIE ✿ STYLE ✿ BEAUTY ✿ LOVE

S

First published in Great Britain in 2017 by Orion Spring,
an imprint of the Orion Publishing Group Ltd
Carmelite House, 50 Victoria Embankment, London, EC4Y 0DZ

An Hachette UK Company

1 3 5 7 9 10 8 6 4 2

A CIP catalogue record for this book is available from the British Library.

ISBN: 9781409170235

Photography: Peter Pedonomou
Design: Smith & Gilmour
Styling: Annie Swain, Sophie Kirkwood and Leigh Williams
Food styling: Iona Blackshaw
Hair and make-up: Lyndsey Harrison
With thanks to Gemma Calvert

Every effort has been made to ensure that the information in the book is accurate.
The information in this book may not be applicable in each individual case so it is
advised that professional medical advice is obtained for specific health matters and
before changing any medication or dosage. Neither the publisher nor author accepts any
legal responsibility for any personal injury or other damage or loss arising from the use of
the information in this book. In addition if you are concerned about your diet or exercise
regime and wish to change them, you should consult a health practitioner first.

Every effort has been made to fulfil requirements with regard to reproducing copyright
material. The author and publisher will be glad to rectify any omissions at the earliest
opportunity.

Printed and bound in Germany

The Orion Publishing Group's policy is to use papers that are natural,
and recyclable products and made from wood grown in sustainable forests.
The logging and manufacturing processes are expected to conform to the
environmental regulations of the country of origin.

www.orionbooks.co.uk

CONTENTS

PROLOGUE:
BRIGHT LIGHTS AND NEW BEGINNINGS

NEWS OF THE BAFTA NOMINATION SPREAD ACROSS *THE ONLY WAY IS ESSEX* SET WITH THE SPEED OF LIGHTNING.

The British Academy of Film and Television Arts awards ceremonies are the British equivalent of the Oscars, and the fact that *TOWIE* had been nominated was mega. It was May 2011, seven months after the show had launched on ITV2 in October 2010, and the email from Rachel Hardy in the press office explained that we were up for the YouTube Audience Award, going head to head with television giants like ITV's global winner *Downton Abbey*, *The Killing*, *Big Fat Gypsy Weddings*, *Miranda* and *Sherlock*. It sounds negative but none of us believed we had a hope in hell of winning telly's top gong, but that didn't matter. We felt like winners just for being nominated at such a massive event in the telly calendar, and that day all the girls had only one dilemma: what to wear?! I decided on a silver sweetheart-neckline flower appliqué frock I'd been promised from one of my favourite brands, Dynasty – but then something terrible happened.

I got the email . . .

It landed in my inbox on the morning of 16 May 2011, one day after Rachel's message about the amazing BAFTA news, and it was from our creative director, Tony Wood. 'I'm afraid space is extremely limited and our allocation has been quickly filled,' he wrote before explaining that there was only room for cast members who had been on *TOWIE* since episode one.

I was heartbroken. My boyfriend and fellow castmate James 'Arg' Argent and all the others including Sam Faiers, Jessica Wright, Nanny Pat and Amy Childs were on the guest list, but as I'd joined later in the series I was no longer eligible to attend.

Feeling crushed, I typed my response to Tony.

'No problem,' I wrote. 'I understand. Lydia.'

Two days later I discovered some shocking news. One of the other cast members, Joey Essex, was on the guest list despite joining the show in series two.

'I've been in it longer than Joey! Going to the BAFTAs is my dream!' I sobbed to my mum later that evening, back at our family home in Woodford Green, Essex.

With that, Mum thrust her chair back from the oak kitchen table.

'No, Lydia. You are going to the BAFTAs,' she said, fetching her laptop.

Tony, who's had tons of experience producing programmes like *Coronation Street* and *Hollyoaks*, was about to receive an email he'd never forget. Debbie Douglas, as all *TOWIE* viewers will know, is as frank and fierce as they come.

'I am disgusted . . . My daughter's given everything to the show . . . What an insult . . . Lydia's been on *TOWIE* since series one . . . She's given it everything . . . All the ups and downs in her relationship . . . This is an outrage' were some of the highlights of Mum's message.

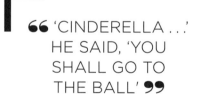

66 'CINDERELLA . . .' HE SAID, 'YOU SHALL GO TO THE BALL' 99

The following day I got a call from Tony. 'Cinderella . . .' he said, 'you SHALL go to the ball.'

I was with Mum at the time. We started jumping around and then she said the annoying thing that all mums do: 'See, I told you, I told you so!'

Before her email I'd begged her: 'Please don't do it. I don't want you to stir up bad feeling between me and the bosses.' But when I bumped into Tony Wood at the *TV Choice* Awards in September 2016, he asked 'How's your lovely mum?' and we ended up in hysterics remembering Mum's email. 'I love the fact she's so honest,' he admitted. 'Straight after she sent me that email I got in touch with the seniors at Lime Pictures and said you had to go.'

Four days later our BAFTA night kicked off early with champagne at the apartment of my co-star Mark Wright. Lime Pictures, the television production company behind *TOWIE*, had organised for hair and make-up artists to get us BAFTA-ready, so by the time James, Mark, his new fiancée Lauren Goodger, Jessica, Nanny Pat and I emerged two hours later we were looking and feeling amazing.

Our first stop was the Gore Hotel in London's Queen's Gate, a gorgeous boutique hotel 20 miles out of Essex, where we met Amy, Sam, Kirk Norcross and Joey for pre-drinks. Everyone was buzzing with excitement. It was the biggest showbiz event we'd ever been to! When it was time for us to head to the awards we were in for another surprise. Lime had pulled out all the stops again, this time with our transport. Generally TV producers are on quite tight budgets but Lime went all out for the BAFTAs – it was a huge celebration of all the hard work paying off. I think we all enjoyed showing the industry we were serious contenders for the award. They laid on a fleet of cars to chauffeur us to the Grosvenor House Hotel on Park Lane where the awards were being held, and every motor was picked to suit our individual personalities.

Amy and Kirk arrived in a fun bright pink Hummer, Joey and Sam cruised in driving a soft-top Mini (a bit like Ken and Barbie) and Nanny Pat rode in an old-fashioned horse-drawn carriage (carrying one of her legendary sausage plaits), and caused a right kerfuffle in central London, bringing rush-hour traffic to a standstill. She was so fretful by the time she arrived at Grosvenor House that she rushed straight in, ditching the sausage plait in the carriage! Mark and Lauren made their way in a modern (and uber swanky) white Rolls-Royce Phantom. And Arg and I were in a classic Rolls-Royce because of my obsession with vintage fashion. Driving through London I felt like Arg and I were newlyweds. I looked like a bride in my dress (which I got to keep), James was in a tux, and we were in the most glamorous motor I'd ever seen. We took selfies the whole way! When we got to the red carpet there were cameras everywhere and they all wanted our photo because we were definitely the most dressed-up bunch on the guest list. I was shaking like a leaf. I'd never had so much press attention and it was so scary because it was our first red-carpet event. I only calmed down when the girls from *Big Fat Gypsy Weddings* turned up. Their outfits were on a whole other level – bright neon dresses adorned with sequins and butterflies and the biggest hairdos I'd ever seen – so the paparazzi attention switched to them. Phew!

The awards were presented by Graham Norton, and when he introduced the *Inbetweeners* actors Simon Bird, Joe Thomas and Blake Harrison to announce the nominations for our category it seemed pretty obvious we hadn't won, because none of the cameras were pointed towards us, and at live award shows winner reactions are critical.

But then something unreal happened.

'And the winner is . . . *The Only Way Is Essex*!' announced Joe. Our two *TOWIE* tables erupted with the volume of a crowd at a One Direction concert, and as we screamed the house down everyone else in the room had faces like thunder, including, I later spotted when I watched it on telly, *Sherlock* actor Benedict Cumberbatch.

Some people say the YouTube Audience Award isn't a real BAFTA because it's decided by a public vote and not the BAFTA committee, but I'd argue that makes it the most important award of all because votes are cast by those who truly count – the viewers.

Everyone ran on stage but I walked up arm-in-arm with Nanny Pat and helped her up the stairs, so I could only grab a position at the edge of the group. Even in the official photo I'm stood behind Sam and Amy, struggling to peek through, but I didn't massively mind because at that time I still felt like a newcomer compared to the rest, since I'd only started at the end of series one.

Mark, ever the professional, gave a speech that he'd been rehearsing for days. 'We're absolutely overwhelmed to even be invited tonight, even nominated, but to win it . . . It's incredible,' he said, and then Amy Childs grabbed the microphone and screeched 'Shuuuuuut upppp!' The audience was embarrassingly silent. The *TOWIE* crowd had brought a whole new atmosphere to the BAFTAs and it was clear that many weren't sure how to take us. But I knew one thing – I was proud to be representing Essex.

That BAFTA win marked the beginning of the rest of my life as I know it. From then on *TOWIE* was the word on everyone's lips and as the programme's notoriety soared, so did our individual profiles. The cast of *TOWIE* were fast becoming stars in their own right, and with fame came a future filled with television appearances, magazine photoshoots and advertising campaigns. *TOWIE* was delivering me success that I'd never ever dreamed could be mine . . .

#1
LIFE BEFORE *TOWIE*

GOOD THINGS COME TO THOSE WHO WAIT, OR SO THE SAYING GOES. THEY ALSO, AS MY PARENTS DISCOVERED ON 20 JANUARY 1991 AT WHIPPS CROSS HOSPITAL IN LEYTONSTONE, REWARD THOSE WHO DON'T . . .

It was 2.05 a.m. on a freezing-cold Sunday when I made my grand entrance into the world, just over two hours after Mum's first breath-stealing contraction. I was also hot on the tail of my elder sister, Georgia, who had popped out 13 months ahead of me. Yes, you read that right, *13* months, which means Mum fell pregnant with me when her first baby was only four months old.

Not intentionally of course. Mum and my dad Dave, a tiler with piercing blue eyes and a wicked sense of humour, took a year to get lucky with Georgia and had even been prescribed a fertility drug called Clomid to shimmy things along. Conceiving again seemed as unlikely as winning the lottery.

Officially, I was an accident but, as Mum maintains, a happy one. Faced with raising two babies under the age of two, many women would (understandably) curl up into a hormone-packed ball of stress, but Mum was rather excited by the idea of her two babies being only a year apart. It would be just like her relationship with her sister, my Auntie Jacqueline, who is only 18 months older than her and is her best friend in the world.

To everyone in Wanstead, east London, where my parents lived at the time, Mum had broken a Guinness World Record during her pregnancy with me. 'Everyone thought I was still pregnant with the first baby,' Mum once told me. 'They'd say, "Haven't you had that baby yet?!"' It was the longest pregnancy in history.

One old nursery rhyme reckons that those born on a Sunday are bonny and blithe and good and gay – in other words pretty and happy. I'm definitely a glass half full kind of person, but I arrived with olive skin and a mass of jet-black hair, which quickly prompted Dad to ask Mum if I really belonged to him! He was only joking, as Dad often does.

I'd been alive for just two weeks when Mum realised there was something desperately wrong with me. Whenever she breastfed me I'd latch onto the boob then start suffocating. I couldn't inhale through my nose when my mouth was rammed against her boob, and the midwife instructed Mum to get me to the health clinic quickly for assessment. There they gave Mum special drops to drip in my nose before every feed, but as I got older my nose was always bunged up and I was a very poorly child, constantly battling colds and flu.

One Christmas, I think I was four, the entire family descended on a huge rented house in Brighton for the holidays and I ended up in bed with a cough but overnight began struggling to breathe. An emergency doctor was called and he diagnosed me with pneumonia, prescribed some antibiotics and instructed my parents to keep me very warm. I remember nothing of this but Mum tells me all I cared about was Father Christmas not coming down our chimney in case he caught the lurgy and me ruining Christmas for kids all over the world.

❀ Child's play ❀

Home, until I turned seven, was a three-bedroom house in Wanstead – part of Essex until 1965 when Greater London was created – where a pink blossom tree grew in the front garden and next door a little boy called Max bounced on an outdoor trampoline that was so big I was sure all the kids in the neighbourhood could squeeze onto it at once. Mum once told me that Max was allowed a trampoline because he was an only child, so at night, lying on the bottom bunk in the pink-painted room I shared with Georgia, I tried to imagine life as an only child. It was impossible . . .

I was 13 months old when Mum started fostering children and since then I've had over 200 brothers and sisters. Mum wasn't always a foster carer. She began her career in the City as a buyer for Debenhams and eventually worked for another big fashion house, but once Georgia and I came along she needed a job she could do from home.

Her 'Eureka!' moment came in 1993 over lunch at Pizza Hut in Stanford Hill, when she sparked up a conversation with a lady on the next table who was looking after six kids. She turned out to be a foster carer and Mum, who's always loved children, was inspired. Within 24 hours Mum was in touch with Hackney social services enquiring about becoming a foster carer herself.

The next stage was for Mum and Dad to go through a detailed assessment, then Mum did a 12-week fostering course, and eight months later they took in their first child, a three-month-old baby girl called Nadia.

In those days, Mum did a lot of short-term foster placements. She'd rush out in the dead of night, drive to one of any number of local police stations, and return home with children whose parents had been arrested, or worse. Some would be with us for a few nights, others only a few hours, but either way Mum's role in their lives was pivotal.

One evening, Mum walked through the door with a bundle in her arms, and snuggled in the white blankets was a baby boy. The next morning I was so excited I jumped out of bed and raced into his bedroom for another look, but nothing could have prepared me for what I saw. 'Mum!' I screamed from across the landing in a blind panic. 'Something's wrong with the baby . . . He's turned

Every family has a story to tell, welcome to ours

(Anonymous)

into a she!' It emerged that in the few hours I'd been sleeping, Mum had returned the boy to the police station and been asked to take in another baby – this time a little girl.

Mum now admits that she often worried about the effect her fostering was having on Georgia and me. Perhaps she thought we'd be emotionally affected by her not giving us her full attention, or by the constantly changing stream of brothers and sisters who we grew to love, then lost. In the beginning, I bawled my eyes out when little ones I'd grown close to suddenly weren't there anymore, but over time 'goodbye' became the norm. Weirdly, for a child, I learned the art of detachment.

And the great truth is, the foster kids slotted perfectly into my creative world. I've always had a wild imagination. As a little girl I dreamed of being a vet like James Herriot and loved nothing more than turning my bedroom into an animal surgery – one day I even ripped the antennae off my ghetto blaster and used it as a 'syringe' to inject my cuddly-toy patients with life-saving medicine. With my new foster brothers and sisters, I could play Mums and Dads with the babies and Secret Garden in the overgrown bottom section of the garden with the older kids. But my favourite game of all was Libraries, where we'd peruse the contents of the bookshelf before taking our chosen reads to a desk where Georgia, the librarian, stamped the first page. Ruthlessly, she also fined us 5p if we returned the book late. I loved writing too and spent hours tucked away in my bedroom writing stories, or with my head buried in an Enid Blyton, Jacqueline Wilson, *Black Beauty* or Aesop's Fables book. Harry Potter was massive at the time but it didn't appeal to me because I've always been exceptionally girlie – even in my bedtime reading!

As amazing as it was growing up in a bustling household full of kids, I sometimes found the chaos overwhelming. I loved family parties and crowds but was a naturally quiet child and felt the happiest when in my own company. I'm exactly the same today.

Funny and fond memories from my childhood

1 When I was a pupil at Chigwell Row Infant School, for months I had a secret that was eating away at me. One lunchtime I was munching on an orange, and as we'd just learned about growing plants in science class I buried some of the seeds in the playground garden. Every day for weeks I went to the water fountain, filled my mouth and secretly spat the water onto the soil, hoping the seeds would one day grow into an orange tree. Not long after, when my parents sold our house in Wanstead, we moved to Woodford Green and I changed schools to Wells Primary. I remember lying awake at night in a cold sweat, thinking: 'What if a tree grows through the middle of the school and destroys the entire building?' As far as I'm aware, Chigwell Row is still standing!

2 When I was younger I loved the Spice Girls, and dancing. I joined my first dance school at the age of six and in primary school I formed a pop group with my best friends Simone, Alex , Kate and Lizzie called the Groove Girls. We performed in school talent shows and I can still remember one of the songs we wrote, which included the lines 'Talent and grooviness, that is what we've got. / It is getting late and we still are looking hot.' I know what you're thinking: had *The X Factor* been around then we'd have been a surefire hit! In 2002, long before *The X Factor* was even a twinkle in Simon Cowell's eye, ITV's *Pop Idol* became a national obsession. Over 10 million viewers were tuning in every Saturday night. For me, the big draw was Gareth Gates, whose boy-next-door looks, stutter and angelic voice stirred feelings in me that I'd never had before. He was my first big crush and when he lost to Will Young in the final I cried for hours. My poor Gareth, how was he going to cope?

3 Growing up I spent a lot of time at my grandparents' house and I loved it there because I was the apple of my nanny and grandad's eye and they spoiled me rotten. We often spent summer evenings in the mini home that Grandad created for me where we loved playing games. I Spy was my favourite. One time, Grandad said: 'I spy with my little eye something beginning with R.' 'Rocks?' suggested Nanny. 'No,' said Grandad. 'Roses!' I shouted. 'Guess again,' replied Grandad. 'Roof?' said Nan, but Grandad shook his head. After 30 minutes Nan and I gave up. 'I knew you would never get it,' laughed Grandad. 'It's . . . red!' Nan was furious. 'You've ruined the game!' she shouted. 'Red isn't a thing, it's a colour!' I was in stitches. You could always count on Grandad to cause a stir, even playing I Spy!

Four years ago I had a psychic reading and I went in feeling very cynical. 'I've got the spirit of an older man here,' said the psychic lady. 'He's laughing and saying the word "red".' I couldn't believe it. I felt very comforted by what she said and I now feel that my grandad is always around.

4 In Porto Recanati where we always holidayed as a family there's a restaurant called Mario's, and when I was seven I had a crush on the owner Mario's nephew Andrea, who was three years older than me. I'd get so nervous around him, and whenever he played on the pinball machine I'd saunter over to hang around him but would be permanently mute. Andrea is now a lifeguard at the beach by day and he still works in the restaurant in the evening. And guess what: I still get nervous when I see him now! I've had a crush on him for my whole life!

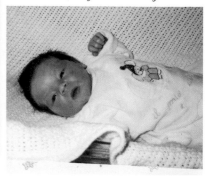

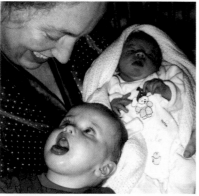

Nanny Maureen and Mum

🌑 My great escape 🌑

One day our house was packed with social workers, guardians, independent reviewers and physiotherapists, so I decided to disappear. An hour or so later Mum found me playing alone in my bedroom wearing a pair of wellington boots, a tutu and pearls, lost in my own world.

My favourite retreat of all was to the Essex village, Stanford Rivers, where my mum's parents Maureen and Romano lived. Nanny Maureen was just 16 when she married my grandad, an Italian painter and decorator with a passion for cigarettes, red wine and gambling. He came to England when he was 14, and we all called him Grandad Lou (after my dad nicknamed him Luigi, which, said Dad, was the most Italian name he knew).

Every Friday afternoon after school, before *Home and Away* came on the telly at 5.10 p.m., I'd sit on the stairs in the hallway, suitcase packed, and wait for my grandad's black Citroën to roll onto the driveway. That car was so embarrassing. Grandad had somehow splattered white paint up the doors, the seats were broken, and there was a huge ladder tied precariously to the roof. But that battered-up Citroën was my ticket out of the craziness of our family home.

Nanny and Grandad's three-bedroom house was in a village as idyllic as any imagined by Enid Blyton. The garden was filled with rose bushes and oversized rhododendrons and at the bottom was a little duck pond, but the best thing of all was the outhouse that Grandad had converted into a miniature home for me and Georgia – complete with French windows, tea lanterns and a floral-patterned sofa. Luckily, I was the golden grandchild and Georgia, perhaps sensing the favouritism or simply wanting a break from her irritating younger sibling, rarely joined me.

My other favourite escape was to Porto Recanati, near Ancona in Italy, where Mum had holidayed as a child. She wanted us to experience what she had so from when I was six months old it became our holiday destination for six glorious weeks of the year. Mum still takes off there every summer to visit our family. I love it there, and now I'm older I really appreciate the culture and the beauty of the area. As kids, Georgia and I spent every minute outdoors lapping up the golden sunshine, the freedom and – as we got older – the Italian boys who went crazy for our blue eyes and blonde hair. They'd pedal their bikes over to our apartment, shout our names and beg us to come out to play. Needless to say, the local girls didn't like us too much – I think they were jealous of us stealing the boys' attention!

66 EVERY YEAR I HAD A 'HOLIDAY ROMANCE', WHICH WAS ALL VERY INNOCENT AND INVOLVED NOTHING MORE THAN HANGING OUT WITH ONE BOY AND SOMETIMES HOLDING HANDS 99

Every year I had a 'holiday romance', which was all very innocent and involved nothing more than hanging out with one boy and sometimes holding hands. As I got older, my best friend from school, a girl called Ilaria Aronne, who, like me, was massively studious, joined us for the trip, and on the plane home we'd play the 'what if' game. Ilaria would say, 'Lydia, what if Alessandro came out the toilet right now and said, "Lydia, come and live with me in Italy forever"?' I've always been a romantic, which might explain why my first kiss at the age of 11 was a bit of a disappointment.

It was one of those weird lunch breaks when there's a mass kiss-off behind the bike shed. Everyone had started experimenting with kissing. Everyone but me. I was too scared – until Peter Feruge, a small boy with glasses, stole my shoe and wouldn't give it back unless I locked my lips on his. Thankfully I got my shoe back, but I can't remember a single thing about the kiss that Peter bribed me into. True romance, hey?

🌹 Grand designs 🌹

Growing up, we never lived in one house for long. Mum and Dad were pros at buying clapped-out properties, renovating them and selling them on to make thousands of pounds of profit, and this work-for-reward mentality is something that's massively influenced my attitude to earning a living. My earliest memory of Dad is him coming in from work with grout all over his hands and mud under his fingernails. He could shower a hundred times but could never get the grout off his fingers, which were covered in cuts and as chunky as pork sausages. Dad used to say: 'Lyd, these are real men's hands.' Those hands got us onto Monkham's Avenue, a beautiful estate in Woodford Green where everyone dreamed of moving to.

Our house was a Tudor-style black-and-white semi-detached four-bedroom property, set over three floors with a massive monkey puzzle tree in the garden. It was also a total wreck. Buckets were scattered all over the floor to catch water from the leaking roof, and we couldn't afford a boiler so we had to bathe at my nan's or Mum would boil the kettle and fill up a big plastic tub in the kitchen.

When we moved in I was nine and mum was nine months pregnant with my younger brother Freddie, who, like me and my sister Romana who followed three years later, was a happy accident. One afternoon Mum was balancing on the top rung of a ladder painting the ceiling with white emulsion when liquid began dripping onto the floor.

'Call Dad!' Mum shouted to me. 'My waters have broken.' I didn't have a clue what she was talking about but figured there was an emergency with our newly fitted roof, so I called Dad's mobile to break what I thought was bad news and told him to come home quick. Everything ended up all right though, because that day Mum gave birth to a baby boy. Our roof didn't need fixing either, which was a right result.

🌹 Sisters of (no) mercy 🌹

Although Woodford Green is full of good secondary schools, Mum was hell-bent on Georgia and me travelling an hour every day to the Anglo European School in Ingatestone, an international school famous for its languages and above-average exam results.

I quickly proved myself to be one of the brainiest in my class. I learned French, German and a little bit of Russian and was one of 20 in my year to enroll in the government's Young, Gifted and Talented Programme, which helps advanced students (I got five As and five Bs in my GCSEs. Whoop!) go the extra mile.

It was a different story with Georgia . . .

Georgia is now my business partner, my travelling buddy, my psychologist (we talk to each other about EVERYTHING) and my best friend, but growing up we were arch-enemies. I hated

❝ I CAN HONESTLY SAY MY SISTER IS MY BEST FRIEND ❞

Georgia for many reasons and it all started from when I was a baby. One time Georgia tried to wrench me out of my pram in the park. On another occasion she spotted me in my baby bouncer, which Mum hung from the kitchen door when she was doing cleaning and washing, and pulled the harness back so far I swung head first against the door, into the wall and back again. Like a human wrecking ball. Georgia never really hurt me but she was very reckless and Mum really shouted at her that day. In fact, Mum shouted at Georgia for her whole childhood because she was so naughty. It's no wonder Mum says she was so protective of me growing up. She had to be!

Georgia was like Dennis the Menace, always up to trouble, usually with me as her plaything. If she wasn't attempting death by pillow suffocation she was giving bath-time drowning a good shot. Whenever we played together we ended up fighting. I just didn't get her back then, which was sad considering we were so close in age.

Georgia would often fly into fits like a wild, caged animal, screaming, shouting and lashing out. I was scared of her my entire life – until the day we were in the biscuit aisle at Morrisons and I hit her! She was picking on me (again) and finally, after fifteen years, I'd had enough of being intimidated. When I slapped her across the face Georgia was stunned into silence, and from that moment our relationship drastically improved. I think she finally realised I was no longer a walkover.

Luckily my sister has mellowed with age. She's still feisty and has a no-nonsense attitude, which probably explains why she makes such a successful business partner, but her fighting, rebellious days are over. Now I can honestly say my sister is my best friend and we often laugh about our volatile past.

Girl gone (temporarily) bad

Although I was a high achiever at school, I was also in the 'it' group, the cool group, which meant I mixed with girls who were naughty and sometimes ended up in trouble too.

'What's Georgia done this time?' sighed Mum when Mrs Martin, my head teacher, telephoned the house shortly after 1 p.m. on a cold Monday one October.

But Mrs Martin replied, 'It's not Georgia. It's Lydia. She is extremely drunk.'

Mum, who told me the story later, began weeping into the handset.

'Don't cry,' soothed Mrs Martin. 'Just get to the school.'

Welcome to the day I first tried alcohol.

I was 14 and a handful of kids were sneaking booze into

With my friend,
Ilaria, in Italy

Me aged eight in
the bucket bath!

school to experiment at lunchtime. Looking back it was so stupid, but because all my friends were doing it I didn't want to be the odd one out. In any case, I thought: 'What harm can come of it? Surely nobody can get *that* drunk on a few sips of alcohol.'

That afternoon behind the sports hall we glugged mouthfuls of Jack Daniel's whiskey, oblivious to the CCTV cameras beaming our every rebellious move into the head's office, where a few minutes later I was stood, swaying.

'I can smell alcohol on your breath,' spat Mrs Martin.

'No Miss, it's Cherry Airwaves chewing gum. It just smells of alcohol,' I replied. The whiskey was making my vision fuzzy and my words slurry. Who was I kidding?

Not Mrs Martin. She suspended me for five days on the spot.

I'd failed Mrs Martin, failed Mum and failed myself. It was a horrendous feeling. Was I now as bad as Georgia? The prospect reduced me to floods of hysterical tears.

By the time Mum arrived to collect me I must have looked like those girls you see in the papers at the end of a night out during university freshers' week. Black mascara was smeared across my tear-stained cheeks and Maybelline Dream Matte Mousse foundation had run onto the collar of my school shirt.

Somewhat surprisingly, Mum didn't shout at me. Instead she enveloped me in a hug, walked me to the car and when we got home she washed my face with baby wipes then put me to bed.

❀ First love dramz ❀

Mum and I have only ever come to big blows a handful of times. Our first big argument (you guessed it) was about a boy.

I was 15 and besotted with my first crush, a guy two years my senior (let's call him Connor) who was from Maldon and was the coolest guy not only in the school but on planet Earth. Connor was also partial to smoking a bit of marijuana, so I kept our romance hidden from my parents who I knew wouldn't approve, and we dated in secret for three months until my maths teacher, Mr Haines, blew it.

'Lydia is on the wrong path,' he announced to Mum during one parents' evening, before filling her in on Connor's extra-curricular interests.

On the car journey home Mum went mental and insisted I finish with Connor. She wasn't worried about me smoking marijuana – she knew I'd seen too much drug-fuelled pain among her foster children to dare try it – but believed I deserved better and began regularly grounding me to stop us seeing each other.

Connor was desperate for us to sleep together, and although some of my friends had started having sex at 15, I wasn't ready. In any case, it was illegal, and I was adamant that I wouldn't be doing any such thing until I hit the legal age of 16.

This didn't sit well with Connor. One night, when I was grounded, he went to a house party and slept with a girl called Sophie and when I confronted him about it in the playground on Monday he didn't deny it.

'You're a frigid fridge freezer,' said Connor, coolly. 'It's over.'

I was utterly devastated, but my advice to any girl being pressured by a guy to lose her virginity is to never do anything you're not ready for. It's your virginity and you can never get it back when it's gone. Treat it like your best friend.

As it goes, I waved goodbye to my 'best friend' just after my 16th birthday with a boy who wore black Ecko tracksuits – the epitome of cool at the time – and put on funny camp accents which made me laugh. Humour has always been the key to my heart, and in this instance it was also the key to a little bit more because six months into dating Ecko boy I slept with him. It was the most painful experience of my life. I hated every minute so we only did it a handful more times before it was over.

❀ Arg on the scene ❀

By the time I left school at 18 my A-level grades were miles off the straight As I'd been predicted. I pulled in two Cs (further maths plus economics and business) and one B (English language) and my parents were as disappointed as I was. We all knew I could have done better and we all knew why I hadn't – James 'Arg' Argent.

James and I had met at a summer polo match and I was head over heels in love, and was in the midst of a new lifestyle, namely partying at a club called Faces on a Thursday, where James ran a night called Liaison. I'd achieved just enough grades-wise to squeeze onto an English language course at Brighton University, but by this point I'd lost interest in studying, didn't want to leave Arg behind to start a new life by the sea and was confused as hell about my future life plan.

Leaving school during a recession like the one that hit Britain in 2008 is rubbish for both your bank balance and your self-esteem. Jobs were non-existent, so I signed up with a temping agency who secured me a job working as a receptionist at a pilot training centre in Heathrow – which was so dull I lasted just three months. By the time James and I were on holiday in Marbella in August 2009 (we travelled with our own groups of friends but spent most of the time together) I was in an equally brain-numbing job, working on reception at an architecture firm, and was desperate for a change.

'I can't go home to work in any more dead-end jobs,' I announced to Arg from my sun lounger on Puerto Banús's Plaza Beach, two days before our holiday was over. 'I worked so hard at school and now I'm wasting my life. I need to do something that makes me happy.'

Yoko Ono, John Lennon's wife, once said: 'A dream you dream alone is only a dream. A dream you dream together is reality.' And at that moment James and I made our first big decision as a couple – to quit England and move to the bright lights of Marbella!

Within two weeks of returning home from holiday we'd caught a one-way flight to Malaga, rented an old-fashioned but perfectly located portside apartment, and, to quote the Human League, I was working as a waitress in a cocktail bar – a venue called The Lounge, near Wayne Lineker's famous bar.

I spent my days sunbathing and my nights serving Sex on the Beach cocktails to punters, but Arg struggled to get work and pretty soon we were rowing more often than we were making up.

I think he resented me for being so happy and in a job I loved.

66 WE DECIDED TO QUIT ENGLAND AND MOVE TO THE BRIGHT LIGHTS OF MARBELLA! 99

I had lots of friends too, and he didn't, so I think he was getting lonely as well as not being able to find work. With me working nights we spent weeks like passing ships in the night, barely seeing each other – and when we did we rubbed each other up the wrong way.

One Sunday James and I went to a champagne spray party at the Ocean Beach Club with a few of his mates who were visiting from Essex. Spray parties are lavish pool parties where the young and beautiful hire oversized beds to lounge on and get smashed on Veuve Clicquot, which they pretend they can afford but secretly can't.

By the end of the afternoon, slightly intoxicated, I left for a shift at The Lounge, leaving behind plenty of guys and girls hooking up. One couple, I later discovered, was James and a rather attractive mystery redhead. Just like in Essex, no secret stays sacred for long in Marbella, and by the morning I'd been fully briefed by a mate from The Lounge who'd seen James and the girl snogging in the water.

I wasted no time in chucking James out the flat. I was over us and had no intention of being with a boy who would betray and humiliate me. A few weeks later James was back in the UK and appearing on a new ITV2 reality show called *The Only Way Is Essex*. Out in Spain I'd seen a few trailers featuring James's best friend Mark Wright, plus a few other well-known Essex faces. People were calling it the UK's answer to *The Hills*, a fly-on-the-wall documentary drama set in LA that had made people like Lauren Conrad and Spencer Pratt world-famous stars.

Little did I know that *TOWIE* would soon change my life in more ways than I could ever imagine . . .

#2
THE ESSEX GIRL DONE GOOD

66 WE REALLY WANT YOU ON THE SHOW. JAMES IS ON BOARD AND IS ADAMANT YOU'RE GOING TO GET BACK TOGETHER. HE WON'T STOP TALKING ABOUT YOU. ARE YOU INTERESTED? **99**

The voice on the line belonged to a woman called Liz who was a cast recruiter at Lime Pictures, one of the UK's leading TV production companies.

I couldn't believe my luck. Since splitting from James my Marbella bubble had truly burst. The summer season was drawing to a close, I'd been kicked out of the flat for subletting a room to my best friend Danielle Park-Dempsey and, more to the point, I was crazily heartbroken. I wanted to return home to Essex and *TOWIE* seemed like a good enough excuse, but I was nervous. What if *TOWIE* was a flop? What if I was made into a laughing stock? What if James wanted to date another girl under my nose? What ifs can rule your world if you're not careful.

'Nothing ventured, nothing gained,' advised Mum, standing in our kitchen back home when I telephoned to offload my confusion. I could hear the hiss of the kettle so I knew she'd be making a brew in the teapot she covers with the purple tea cosy that Nan knitted her. 'Good old Mum,' I thought. 'Always in favour of living the dream.' Mum's motto in life has always been 'Go for it!' so my dilemma about joining *The Only Way Is Essex* was quickly resolved.

Liz, a blonde lady in her 30s, was soon in Marbella armed with a little video camera, which she used to hoover up test footage of me hanging out with Danielle, who later joined *TOWIE* herself. She was obviously assessing how I looked and acted on camera, and I could tell that she was impressed.

The morning I missed my flight home after getting drunk at my Marbella leaving party Liz called to tell me that I was in. The producers were thrilled with the footage and had offered me a part on the show, to start straight away. They offered to fund my journey home, including all my excess baggage, and with no money to pay for another flight it was this that sealed the deal for me. In any case, I figured I didn't have anything to lose. 'If it ends tomorrow at least it's a tale for the grandkids,' I thought.

◉ Lights, camera . . . action! ◉

Within four days of landing back in Essex I was in Chigwell's King William IV pub, deep-diaphragm breathing ahead of my knee-knockingly scary *TOWIE* debut.

Everyone seems to think my first scene was me walking up to James in the Kings Oak Hotel at a beauty spot in Epping Forest called High Beech. That was actually my second appearance on the show. My first moment was teasing up that scene alongside one of my best friends from my neighbourhood, a girl called Ellie Redman, who had Spanish heritage and worked as a receptionist up the City.

Mum helped me get ready for my screen debut. She loaned me a green vintage cape, which I teamed with a crisp white shirt and black cigarette trousers, and I felt super confident about my look.

The producers told me that for my first scene I needed to walk across the restaurant where I'd bump into someone who would invite me to a party. That someone was James's friend Mark Wright, who was propping up the bar with a stunning brunette from Brentwood who he introduced as Lucy. I later found out her full name was Lucy Mecklenburgh, and for months I couldn't pronounce her surname! What I did know was that Lucy was the most insanely beautiful girl I'd ever met, and it was no surprise that she was with Mark, who has always had a taste for gorgeous women.

Even when the cameras were rolling my nerves still didn't go away, and it took me a long time to get comfortable being filmed. Some people fit straight in to working in television, like one of the newest stars, Amber Dowding, who I think is a natural.

By the time of my first scene with James a couple of days later we'd met up briefly, and although I'd told him that *TOWIE* producers had been in touch about me joining the show he was in the dark about me being there that day. For two and a half hours before I stepped on set, Ellie and I were holed up in the ladies' toilets. I felt so sick with nerves but I busied myself by touching up my face with Ellie's make-up.

> ❝ IT TOOK ME A LONG TIME TO GET COMFORTABLE BEING FILMED ❞

Anyone who saw my first scene with James will remember that he told me he missed me and wanted me back. By then I'd rationalised that his pool-party kiss hadn't entirely been his fault, that I too had been guilty of neglecting him in Marbella. I partied with my bar mates most evenings after work and was at pool parties during the day, leaving him by himself a lot of the time. But I wasn't about to tell James all this.

'I always used to see myself being with you, but at the moment I don't see anything. Sorry,' I said, giving him a peck on the cheek and walking off. I felt terrible about snubbing James, especially when my heart was screaming at me to kiss him, but I knew I had to be strong. If James wanted me back he was going to have to graft for it.

If we don't change,
we don't grow.
If we don't grow,
we are not
really living

(Gail Sheehy)

In the *TOWIE* bubble

Watching yourself on telly for the first time is seriously weird, but nothing could have prepared me for what I looked like on screen the night my first episode aired. My face was caked in Ellie's two-shades-too-dark make-up and was framed by a mass of overly backcombed hair, which had been sprayed with Elnett to within an inch of its life. I looked like a shiny orange drag queen, and judging by the Twitter backlash the public felt the same. People were also slating me for spurning James who had instantly been embraced as the nation's sweetheart. I had to call James.

'I don't know if I can do this,' I sobbed as James held me in his arms. He'd raced over within minutes of my call.

'You've got to persevere with it. Nobody knows our full story, but they will do,' he replied, before adding: 'I love you, Lydia.'

It was all I needed to hear. By the time we kissed goodbye on my doorstep Lydia and Arg were back together. Twitter could take a running jump.

TOWIE fever quickly took hold, although people were initially confused by the format, primarily wondering how much was real and how much was dramatised. The *TOWIE* format is what we call 'structured reality'. Or 'dramality' – i.e. dramatic reality. If anything happens in our lives, however big or small, we let the *TOWIE* guys know. They call us to discuss ideas and do post-scene catch-ups to talk about how it went and how we feel, which help the producers to draw up a loose running order of what's going to be filmed the next day and where. The night before filming we get allocated a time to meet and a location, and most of the time we know who we're filming with, but if the producers want to create drama they keep that a secret.

Going back to my point about early-days *TOWIE* fever . . . Average viewing figures of 1.4 million plus a healthy audience online proved the programme was going places.

We were, too. Invitations for 'celebrity events' were trickling in, and one of my first was the DVD launch of the *Sex and the City* movie, a glamorous affair hosted in a private champagne lounge above Swarovski on Regent Street.

I'd been on the show less than six months and knew the paparazzi would be there so I had to make an impression. Taking inspiration from Carrie Bradshaw herself I borrowed a Roberto Cavalli floral silk dress from my mum's friend Nicole, who has an enviable wardrobe of designer clothes. When I walked in with Lucy and Sam I felt like the most glamorous person in the building.

I saw him across the room straight away – Willie Garson, the actor who plays Carrie's gay best friend Stanford Blatch – and don't ask what came over me. Before I could blink I was in front of Willie telling him that everyone calls me 'Carrie of Essex' because, like Sarah Jessica Parker's character, 'I love fashion and have a boyfriend who looks a bit like Mr Big'. Willie smiled politely and told me Sarah was 'lovely'. I was so happy.

Afterwards, Sam, Lucy and I caught a cab to Mahiki, a nightclub opposite the Ritz hotel, but were turned away by the bouncers who gleefully informed us of a 'No *TOWIE*' policy. It was the ultimate humiliation and put a real dampener on the night. Even worse, our embarrassing rejection was all over the *Mail Online* the following day.

✿ Seeing stars ✿

One evening that stands out from my early *TOWIE* years was at *The Sun*'s Military Awards. Arg and I were invited in December 2011 and the red carpet at London's Imperial War Museum was like a Who's Who of celebrities – everyone from David Walliams to Peter Andre and the Duke and Duchess of Cornwall was there.

It was a huge night, but my choice of dress was all wrong. I'd been to LA a couple of weeks earlier with Lauren Goodger and had picked up a floor-length cream number complete with sequined detail (just below the crotch) from a vintage store. What I'd originally thought was 'so Florence and the Machine' was actually more 'Lily Savage', and the sequins looked like a giant vajazzle! Thankfully, there was one man inside who instantly distracted me from my fashion faux pas – David Beckham.

'David! Do you watch the show?' said Arg, bowling up to David Beckham when we were inside the event. He was with his sons Brooklyn and Romeo, who were 12 and nine at the time and looked so cute in their miniature suits. A hundred people were queuing up for selfies with David but somehow we slipped to the front, and David was in no hurry to rush us away, which was fortunate because I couldn't take my eyes off him.

'I've been in LA so not had a chance but I've heard so much about it,' replied David. 'I love Essex. I still get my pie and mash from there.' What a guy!

That summer the *TOWIE* cast was invited for the first time to ITV's annual summer party, hosted by the channel's director of television, Peter Fincham, and we were all out in force: James, Lucy, Joey, Sam, Mark, Jessica, Lauren Goodger and I. We were also all bricking it.

Of course, we'd been to celebrity events before but (BAFTAs and Millies aside) usually less industry-heavy ones, such as club openings, product launches and film screenings.

The ITV party was going to be in a different league, packed wall-to-wall with celebrities, so in the car en route to west London Jessica and I were hyperventilating with excitement, while Mark, ever the deep-thinker, hatched a survival plan. We must stick together all night, he insisted, and above all else, not get drunk and make fools of ourselves.

The day I interviewed
Ed Miliband

I was shaking with anticipation as we walked inside, illuminated by the light bulbs of a swarm of paparazzi. In one corner of the room I saw Ant and Dec chatting to Myleene Klass, by the bar I spied Holly Willoughby looking radiant in a fuchsia-pink maxi, and then, out of nowhere, Emma Bunton was striding towards me in a beautiful and bright little red dress and nude heels.

'I love you! You're my favourite on *TOWIE* – you're brilliant!' she smiled, grabbing my hand like I was her best friend.

'Oh my God, thank you!' I said, confessing that she was my favourite Spice Girl, and I wasn't just being polite. I genuinely had been the biggest Baby Spice fan of all time. I had Spice Girls stickers in my photo albums, I had Spice Girls birthday cakes and I saw *Spice World* in the cinema. I even got tickets to see them at Wembley Arena. I'd been obsessed and here was one-fifth of my favourite band in the world talking to ME!

Arg had bigger fish to fry, namely Peter Fincham. He strode over to the man who was single-handedly responsible for launching all our careers and said: 'Peter! Nice to meet you. Thanks for inviting us.' Then he was in front of Piers Morgan and his heavily pregnant journalist wife Celia Walden.

'Piers! I love what you're doing in America, mate. Listen, my girlfriend's got a bit of a crush on you. Would you mind posing with her for a photo?'

'You've got a crush on me have you?' said Piers, smiling in my direction, as amused as Celia clearly was, judging by her chuckles.

My face went as red as Emma Bunton's dress. 'Yes,' I said. 'I love your posh voice.'

Flattery gets you everywhere because soon Piers was posing for photographs with me, Sam and Jessica.

By the end of the night Jess and Sam were paralytic and departed from Peter Fincham's house with scarves wrapped around their heads like turbans. The paps had a field day and in the car home Mark was furious.

'You can't get drunk at industry parties! We've got to act like we're one of them,' he grumbled as we whizzed through the streets of west London in the direction of the M11.

I agreed, because by then, at the risk of sounding a little self-inflated, my growing reputation as a fashionista – thanks to my passion for vintage clothes – was one I was petrified of ruining. Offers of magazine shoots were already stacking up, including my first cover shoot with *The Sun on Sunday*'s *Fabulous* magazine (oh my gosh, that was so surreal), plus *InStyle*, *Easy Living*, *More!* and *i-D*, one of the industry's most prestigious fashion magazines, founded by *Vogue*'s former art director Terry Jones. Rather amazingly, they cherry-picked me as *TOWIE*'s most fashionable cast member and wanted to celebrate the fact with an exclusive photoshoot. I was flabbergasted but so grateful. Other than *Fabulous*, I'd only previously taken part in shoots for weekly magazines like *Now* and *Closer*, so *i-D* was a different kettle of fish. At the studio in east London the entire clothing rail was packed with designer clothes, and the Chanel jewellery even rocked up with its own security guard!

66 OFFERS OF MAGAZINE SHOOTS WERE ALREADY STACKING UP 99

There was one look on that shoot that made me feel massively out of my comfort zone. I wore a pair of Cavalli jeans and a Jean Paul Gaultier bra and panicked because the bra material was see-through. 'Why do they want to see my nipples?' I wondered but now I get it. It's just *fashion*. Wearing designer brands completely out of my price range and being shot by Nik Hartley, a well-known fashion photographer who also shot for *Vogue*, was a dream I never imagined possible.

Back then none of the cast were paid to appear on *TOWIE* so I was living off the nest egg I'd saved in Marbella, about £4,000 from bar wages and tips. Any money I made from *TOWIE* came from endorsement deals and magazine shoots, but I didn't earn a penny from *i-D*. The payment was all in the prestige, and if they'd have asked me, I would have probably paid them for the opportunity!

◉ Meeting Kirsty ◉

Initially, Lime Pictures was managing all our publicity. I think they were scared of the cast becoming bigger than the show itself, but in early 2012, as *TOWIE* got bigger and bigger, everyone agreed it would be better if we all had individual management.

James was being represented by a bloke called Neil Dobias who worked for a well-known guy in the industry called Dave Read, a strongly after-shaved agent who once represented Katie Price. Although James raved about Dave and Neil we agreed that because of my interest in fashion I needed somebody with contacts in that industry.

Arg got the mobile number for Kirsty Williams, the managing director at Insanity Talent Management, from a member of the ITV press team who was promoting a programme starring Peaches Geldof, one of Kirsty's clients. I really hoped she would be interested in representing me, although I was hesitant about approaching her since she had some really big names on her books.

I'm rubbish at bigging myself up, I find it embarrassing, so I'd definitely be that poor person on BBC Two's *Dragons' Den* who flunks the sales pitch and leaves empty handed. Luckily, when it came to finding management, I had James to lean on.

My life is a performance for which I was never given any chance to rehearse

(Ashleigh Brilliant)

If James wasn't on *TOWIE* he'd be flogging Ferraris in a swanky showroom, or selling ice to Eskimos. Selling me to Kirsty was, he said, going to be easy.

'Hi, Kirsty. This is Arg,' said James when Kirsty picked up the phone.

'Who's Arg?' she replied. Clearly not a *TOWIE* fan.

'James Argent from *TOWIE*. I've got my girlfriend here. She's really into fashion and needs a manager. You've got to meet her.'

Even I was sold. Kirsty called back a few minutes later and a meeting was set up for a few days later at the Insanity offices on Little Portland Street in central London. When we met, Kirsty and I chatted for two hours and I admitted to her that I didn't know where *TOWIE* was going to take me but that I needed help to use the show as a platform to build my fashion credibility. We talked about James, my mum's fostering and our love of animals, and by the end of the week I was signed up to Insanity with Kirsty as my manager.

A manager is responsible for securing you work, and because they manage your diary you end up speaking to them every single day. Kirsty has always been good for me because she was firm with her direction. When *TOWIE* started it was tempting to grab the first opportunities that came along, but Kirsty encouraged me to be selective instead of going for the quick buck. She advised me not to do underwear shoots with newspapers like the *Daily Star* because they could jeopardise other (and better) opportunities. She's been a really good manager because she instilled in me a huge level of professionalism and a strong work ethic. She's also a great girl and we get on really well. I count her as one of my closest friends.

Celebrities I still can't believe I've met

Over the years I've been very lucky to meet a lot of celebrities and some have become dear friends. Meeting mega superstars like David Beckham is always a surreal experience. Here are a few more famous names that deserve a shout out . . .

Nile Rodgers: In June 2016 I was a guest on a Channel 5 programme called *The Saturday Show* alongside comedian Mark Dolan (who I later appeared on Channel 4's *The Jump* with) and *Birds of a Feather* actress Linda Robson. I'd heard of them both but I didn't have a clue who the third guest was, a guy called Nile Rodgers (FYI he's disco royalty), so when he started his interview and began chatting about being mates with Michael Jackson and Madonna I was slack jawed. 'How have I never heard of this guy?' I thought. Backstage after the show I said to Nile: 'You're a superstar!' Heck, he even had an entourage! Then he began asking questions about me so I told him all about *TOWIE* and my business, Bella Sorella, and he said: 'You're such a cool girl.' Talk about amazing! Afterwards Nile tweeted a picture of us saying: 'You are mad cool. Do I need to bring the girls in my band over to your boutique?' Disco royalty was tweeting me! My dad was well impressed. It's just a shame Nile didn't fit a visit to Essex into his schedule.

The Duchess of Cornwall: In May 2016, after being announced as fostering ambassadors for the Department for Education, Mum and I were invited to Buckingham Palace for afternoon tea to celebrate 150 years of the charity Barnardo's. We didn't meet the Queen but we did shake hands with the Duchess of Cornwall. I managed to stutter 'Thank you for hospitality,' getting my words all mixed up. Mum, however, was as cool as a cucumber

and shook Camilla's hand whilst saying 'Love the outfit, Camilla. Love it. Very chic!' You can count on my mum to break the rules, but she was right – Camilla's chic pink two-piece was fabulous. And she was lovely. I felt honoured to meet her.

Gordon Ramsay: In December 2011 my family and Arg were invited to take part in Gordon Ramsay's *Cookalong Live* Christmas special, a show where the public tune in and cook Christmas dinner under the guidance of Gordon. It was a disaster. Mum got over-excited and dropped everything, Arg got all the measurements and instructions wrong and was already merry on champagne before the cameras were running, and the dinner came out nothing like Gordon had anticipated. But the whole thing was hilarious. At a celebrity event a few months later I bumped into Gordon and we had a good laugh about it. It was great to finally meet him and have something funny to talk about!

Richard Branson: In July 2012 I entered the London Virgin Triathlon with my friend, the TV presenter, Zoe Hardman. Never did I think we would actually meet the main man himself, Richard Branson, a businessman I've always admired. A few days before the race, at the pre-event photocall, he was there to greet us and I was bowled over by how fun, youthful, energetic and full of life he was. I guess a net worth of £3.7 billion does that to you! For one picture he even fireman-lifted Zoe! On the day of the race Richard was there again and he even made time to take a photo with my little sister Romana and her friend. They were only nine so they didn't have a clue who he was, but my mum insisted on a snap just so she could meet him too!

🌹 Goodbye, *TOWIE* 🌹

Fast forward 10 months to December 2012 and the *TOWIE* tables had drastically turned, the full details of which I'll explain later. In a nutshell, James and I were over after a year of strife, I was dating my co-star Tom Kilbey, and I felt angry about so many things including seeing James, thanks to fame, turn into a guy I didn't recognise. Furthermore his animosity towards Tom wasn't helping.

I was in the throes of launching my first Lydia Rose Bright fashion collection and had moved into my first property, a gorgeous two-bedroom cottage in Buckhurst Hill, on the same road as my Nanny Maureen. But I was only just 21 and the pressure of it all was becoming too much.

I confided in my best friend on the show, a cast liaison officer called Mike Spencer whose job it was to know everything going on in my life and report it to the show's storyline team. Mike was from a seaside town called Margate; he was super camp, hilarious and really protective of me. Whenever James stepped out of line (this happened a lot before we split) Mike was the mediator, and if I said to him 'Mike, I can't talk about this or that on camera yet' he'd have a quiet word with the producers and tell them to go easy on me.

But Mike's support wasn't enough. I'm not the sort to go over and over my problems with friends or cry and bitch about boyfriends. In fact, I don't actually like offloading because I hate the thought of people feeling sorry for me. On *TOWIE* I was doing all of that and it started to feel like I was sacrificing my integrity for the sake of TV show ratings.

In December 2012 I called a meeting with our executive producer, a lady called Suzanne, and broke the news – I was leaving *TOWIE*.

The first thing I noticed after my goodbye scenes aired in the Christmas special were the party invitations, which arrived thick and fast. PR teams that had previously denied me access to cool, edgy fashion events just because of my association with *TOWIE* were suddenly approaching Kirsty to confirm my name alongside celebrities like fashion blogger Bip Ling and former *Made in Chelsea* star Millie Mackintosh.

My fashion collection, which I launched with Lipstick Boutique, became the third best seller on ASOS, and by June 2013 Bella Sorella had won a prestigious Drapers Award in the 100 Best Independent Retailers category. 'Lydia from *TOWIE*' was fast becoming 'Lydia the designer', and with my fashion credentials growing, I decided that appearing on any other reality TV shows wasn't an option.

Without a hectic *TOWIE* filming schedule I was suddenly able to focus on other ventures that I was passionate about, like my fashion blog and Bella Sorella. I also tried my hand at presenting.

66 I LOVED BEING BACK IN FRONT OF THE CAMERA 99

YouTube was really blowing up at around this time, so I was excited when I was approached to present a 20-episode online show called *Dating Dilemmas* with Jim Chapman, an uber cool vlogger who is also married to British beauty blogger extraordinaire Tanya Burr. The first episode of the show went out in May 2013, and featured daters who went on three dates each week before reporting back to me and Jim. I really enjoyed it. I didn't know anything about the YouTube world before then and it opened my eyes to how huge it is. I loved being back in front of the camera and my dream was to become a TV presenter, so I guess a part of me was hoping that some top producer would give me a chance.

Set your sights high, the higher the better. Expect the most wonderful things to happen, not in the future but right now. Realise that nothing is too good

(Eileen Caddy)

🌀 I want you back 🌀

But after a few months I was missing the regular interaction with *TOWIE* fans, which had been such a big part of my old life. I was proud that I'd taken a leap of faith and tried other things but there was a *TOWIE*-shaped hole in my heart that I couldn't ignore. When you're on location with *TOWIE* it's nuts and it can be stressful, but I love the craziness that the show brings. It's a rollercoaster, but life without *TOWIE* was too quiet.

One afternoon, heading home on the Central line following a spot of retail therapy on Oxford Street, I called Kirsty. 'Kirst, I'm ready to go back to *TOWIE*,' I blurted out when she answered, and we scheduled a meeting for the following day.

I could already imagine the headlines: 'Lydia returns after failing to make it in the real world' or 'Lydia can't cut it without *TOWIE*' and the prospect of being dubbed a flop by media critics was unbearable. The truth is, I knew I wasn't a failure because I'd achieved so much away from the media and the spotlight. I'd worked hard on my collection and my fashion blog (that I still write), opened pop-up shops around the UK and invested precious time into Bella Sorella. And there was no shame in admitting that I loved *TOWIE* and TV being in my life.

When I returned to *TOWIE* I continued to push myself out of my comfort zone with the jobs I secured outside the perimeter of the show's storylines. By the end of the year the general election was fast approaching and I remember thinking: 'I'm not sure what the heck's going on, so if I feel that way thousands of other young people must do too.'

During my time out I'd come up with a format for a TV show to introduce young people to the basics of politics. I pitched the idea to a couple of production companies in the hope it would get commissioned, but disappointingly it didn't. In January 2015, during a charity cycle ride through Vietnam and Cambodia with a group of celebrities including TV presenter Matt Johnson, he told me about a government campaign he was involved with called Use Your Voice. It was aimed at encouraging millennials (that's 20- and 30-somethings FYI) to register to vote.

'You target the market we're aiming at,' Matt pointed out as we pedalled through a city called Siem Reap in north-west Cambodia – and he was right. ITVBe, *TOWIE*'s new channel, has a 16- to 34-year-old demographic, with 39 per cent of its primetime audience falling in this age range.

When we got back to the UK I signed up for the campaign and one part was the #silencechallenge. For three days we posted blank updates and empty photos on Twitter to highlight how young people have no voice if they don't vote, and for a social media fanatic like me it was horrendously tough, particularly when Zayn Malik left One Direction and the entire world was tweeting! Even worse, by the end of day two my Twitter followers were down by 20,000, so people clearly thought my account had been hacked! But it was all for a good cause.

> 66 'I'VE GOT YOU AN INTERVIEW WITH ED MILIBAND,' ANNOUNCED ONE OF THE TV PRODUCTION GUYS 99

'I've got you an interview with Ed Miliband,' announced one of the TV production guys on the final day of the campaign, explaining they wanted me to talk politics with the Labour leader in a way that young people would relate to.

'What? How? When?' I replied, suddenly bricking it. Although I knew who Ed was I was clueless beyond that.

I googled solidly for two days and by the time I was interviewing Ed on a south London council estate, although I was full of flu, I felt confident.

Yes, there were a couple of cringeworthy moments, like when I called Labour 'The Labour', but I never promised to be the next

Jeremy Paxman, did I? Ed was a sweetheart and complimented me for using *TOWIE* as a platform to influence society and my mum for fostering so many kids. He also raved about meeting Joey Essex at a political rally three weeks earlier, and like Joey, who posed for a selfie with Ed, I grabbed one too.

Since then I've appeared on Channel 4's EU referendum debate, which was hosted by Jeremy Paxman.

TOWIE has given me an amazing start in life and I think I'm a lot more grateful to the show than I was before I took time out. I was never a diva, but there were times in the past when I didn't want to film scenes or whinged about the long hours.

My time out was a bit like breaking up with a boyfriend, because I realised that sometimes you need to step away to understand how good you had it in the first place. Which leads me to the next and biggest chapter in my life . . .

#3
ARGENT
PROVOCATEUR

66 THE MOMENT I MET YOU I KNEW YOU WERE SPECIAL. YOU WERE PARALYTIC AND SPRAYED PERFUME IN YOUR MOUTH BUT EVEN THOUGH IT DIDN'T TASTE GREAT I COULDN'T RESIST KISSING YOU AND UNTIL THEN I DIDN'T REALISE HOW DEEPLY I COULD LOVE SOMEONE. **99**

These words are penned inside Arg's first ever Christmas card to me, a gigantic musical extravaganza that arrived in a box instead of an envelope.

James and I met on Saturday 5 July 2008 at the Duke of Essex Polo Trophy, which was held at Epping's swanky Gaynes Park and was the event that every girl and guy in Essex was psyched for.

Nobody cares much about the polo. The Duke of Essex is all about the party after dark when DJs play music in giant swankily decorated marquees and the entire Essex party crowd gets rip-roaring drunk.

I was so excited. I'd paid £50 for my ticket and bought a silver sequinned frock from Dorothy Perkins, but some girls had gone the extra mile. One of my friends even had her boobs done for the occasion!

By now I was 17 and studying at West Hatch, where I'd made two good friends called Robyn and Georgia, whose glamorous elder sisters, Abbie and Chloe, were PAs in the City. I idolised them. Not only did they have professional blow-dries and spray tans and wear false lashes but they had also introduced me to a new and exciting world of socialising. On Thursday nights we'd head to a bar in Buckhurst Hill called Rocky's before hitting Faces nightclub in Gants Hill, and on Fridays we went to a cool pub in Walthamstow called the Rising Sun.

Abbie was also mates with a guy called James Argent, who promoted a night called Liaison at Faces, and that day at the polo he was with his mates Mark Wright and Jack Tweed. They were part of the Essex in-crowd (your ticket in required being gorgeous or having an aspirational lifestyle, or both), a little older than me, and while all the girls fancied his mates, 18-stone, joke-telling Arg was considered more of a cuddly, brotherly type. For Arg – who had a huge crush on my friend Robyn – this wasn't ideal.

I've got a picture of Arg from that night. He's wearing a black suit and has a skinhead, like all the boys did that summer. They'd been inspired by David Beckham who shaved off his locks before moving to LA, but the trend didn't suit poor Arg. His lack of hair only emphasised his large nose. Not the best look!

Ashton Kutcher has always been my dream man. There, I've said it. He's goofy, funny, tall, ridiculously hot. Truthfully, I didn't fancy Arg when we first met and, in any case, he was interested in my mate Robyn, until she started copping off with another guy and Arg turned his sights on me. But by the end of the night I was smashed on Sauvignon Blanc and cracking up at Arg's hilarious banter.

I've no memory of grinding against Arg to Rihanna's 'Umbrella', no memory of pulling a bottle of Versace Red Jeans perfume from my handbag and spraying it in my mouth, mistaking it for breath freshener, and certainly no memory of Arg leaning in for a snog at the end of the night in front of all our friends.

After a horrendously hung-over Sunday shift at Woolworths in South Woodford (where I worked part-time) the following day, my friends gleefully filled in the blanks of the drunken night. 'I don't even fancy him! And in any case, he fancies Robyn,' I said to the girls. Waves of embarrassment about having Robyn's sloppy seconds washed over me, but most of all I was worried. Was Arg spreading rumours that we'd done something more? What the hell had I even said to Arg? I vowed never to drink again and decided there was only one thing for it – I had to speak to him to get some answers.

Three or four days later I Facebooked Arg, and when he replied he told me the kissing rumours were true and seemed pretty happy about it, which he proved at midnight every Thursday thereafter at Faces by smooching my face off in the R&B room.

🌸 Life on Marbs 🌸

That summer I made my first pilgrimage to Marbella, one of the ultimate Essex traditions, on my first ever no-parents holiday.

I'd saved up £350 from working in Woolworths to pay for my share of the accommodation – a five-bedroom villa in swanky Puerto Banús, the glamorous and glitzy port-side town filled with luxury yachts and fancy nightclubs.

What a trip! We spent the days sunbathing by the villa pool and gossiping (usually about our antics of the evening before) and the evenings partying until the early hours on the port.

On the second night, while partying at a club called Tibu, a tall, flash, good-looking boy from Loughton called Henry kept trying it on with me. Soon gossip began filtering home that I was into Henry – and it was all true because one night we had a drunken snog in Tibu and the whole thing was witnessed by Arg's mate (and my future *TOWIE* co-star) Lewis Bloor, who wasted no time in bowling up to me to tell me I was 'bang out of order'.

'You're Arg's girlfriend! What are you doing?' he asked, moments after the snog. I was confused and a bit annoyed to be honest, because Arg and I weren't official. We'd only snogged a few times and had never even been on a date. Who the heck did Lewis think he was?

'Arg is telling everyone that you're an item,' Lewis continued.

When I got back to Essex I called James and was steeled for

an argument. If he did think I was his girlfriend he'd be understandably miffed about my tongue-tennis session with Henry. But instead of ranting, James nervously laughed and then made a declaration.

'Lydia, I really want to see you more. I want to be your boyfriend,' he said, and that night we changed our Facebook statuses to 'in a relationship'. Lydia and Arg were official, which called for a big relationship step: our first official date . . .

'You cannot go on a date with him – he looks like Shrek!' shrieked Mum, typically filter-free, from the top of the stairs as James ambled down the driveway. Bless him. He was on time, dressed smartly in jeans and a canary-yellow M&S jumper, oblivious to the conversation going on inside our house.

66 'LYDIA, I REALLY WANT TO SEE YOU MORE. I WANT TO BE YOUR BOYFRIEND' 99

We'd only been in South Woodford's Odeon cinema for five minutes when I heard a familiar voice coming from a few seats behind. It was a close friend of my mum's and I couldn't remember her name for the life of me.

'Lyd, who are you on a date with? Bananaman?,' laughed the woman, referring to Arg's sweater and making me wish the earth would swallow me up. It's so cruel when people make jokes at another person's expense, but to James it was like water off a duck's back. He just laughed. Poor Arg.

I never planned to fall in love with Bananaman but I didn't have any choice. The feeling started in the cinema when he sang along to every word of the Abba songs in *Mamma Mia!* while gently clasping my hand in the darkness, then later when we plonked down on a bench in front of the Shell petrol station and James ploughed through a packet of salt-and-vinegar Square crisps and a Mars chocolate milkshake. That's when he asked if he could kiss me.

'Of course,' I replied. It seemed a silly question considering we'd snogged so many times in the club, but I found his question really gentlemanly and so romantic. As it goes, sober James is a very good kisser!

The next day he disappeared on a three-week holiday to Miami and I missed him like mad. I racked up a £450 phone bill from speaking to him every day, which caused Dad to go ballistic as he was the one paying for it.

🌹 My surprise Mr Perfect 🌹

Luckily, when James returned, I didn't have to wait long for our second date. He invited me to a football match at Charlton FC to watch Mark's younger brother Josh, who played professionally for Scunthorpe United at the time. Arg offered to pick me up and I squealed a little bit inside when a black Range Rover pulled up outside the house. James was quickly becoming my perfect man and I couldn't wait to be sat beside him, cruising around Essex in his beautiful motor.

When I opened the passenger door I came face to face with Jack Tweed. Mark was driving and Arg was in the back beside another bloke called George Andretti. On the 13-mile journey to Charlton in south-east London, James's mates spilled the beans that James didn't have a driving licence, and nine years later he still doesn't.

'Oi, Arg! Get off the billboard!' bantered Jack as we cruised down the A12 past a giant photo of a supersize Italian man advertising pasta sauce.

'For God's sake,' interjected Mark, sounding serious. 'The match has been called off.'

'Why?' asked Arg.

'The thunder and lightning.' With that Mark let one rip, which the guys thought was hilarious and I found gross. These guys were three years older than me and were acting like kids, but nothing could put me off Arg. I was infatuated, and I had a feeling that he was into me too.

Dating Arg – especially the fact that he was a club promoter – went down well with the other students at West Hatch. Every Thursday queues for his night at Faces were a mile long, but I was able to walk to the front of the line and pass the bouncers without even showing ID. Suddenly the school's coolest girls were clamouring to be my best mate and boys in the year above were begging for queue-jump passes.

Apparently girls are attracted to men who subconsciously remind them of their dads. Well, my dad's best trait is his humour and the same goes for James. Dad's a big comedian and everyone says he looks and sounds like Cockney funny man Micky Flanagan. He's got a dry sense of humour and is always doing silly things. I remember him coming down for breakfast when we were younger with his trousers hoisted higher than Simon Cowell's have ever been and his belly pushed right out. He'd say 'Give us a kiss then!' and attack us with a shower of soppy, wet kisses.

I always secretly hoped I'd end up with a guy as funny as Dad, and it turned out that James was.

Dad was born on a rough council estate in Mottingham, south-east London, to a tiler called Fred Bright and a lady called Joan Peters, otherwise known as Dinky because of her height (or lack of it). Dinky was tragically killed in a car crash when Dad was only three years old, so he was raised by his grandmother, Edie. Too young to cope with the death of his beloved and being a single dad, Fred wasn't always on the scene and Dad, sadly, now has little contact with him or any of his blood relatives, which include a couple of half-siblings.

Dad tells me that before he met Mum in the Royal Albert pub in Deptford, south-east London, he was a bit of a lost sheep.

You will never be able to escape from your heart. So it's better to listen to what it has to say

(Paulo Coelho)

My 5 first date rules

1 **Wear something you'd feel comfortable meeting his parents in.** You never want to walk out the door in anything too funky, revealing or extravagant, so choose an outfit that edges on the side of conservative. Remember, figure-hugging and feminine is fine! You can't go wrong with a black jumpsuit or a knee-length pencil skirt with a cute knit or blouse.

2 **Go for a neutral lip.** Red lips look cool but you might well be indulging in a peck on the lips at the end of the night, so choose a baby-pink lipstick or gloss to avoid embarrassing smudges!

3 **Big up the blow-dry, then make under.** Bouncy hair always looks lovely and will give you a more subtle touch of glamour than OTT make-up. Boys usually say they prefer the 'less is more' approach to make-up, so don't go overboard with cosmetics. If you're going to wear a fake lash choose a natural look rather than a dramatic party lash.

4 **Be the best version of you.** It should go without saying but don't neck three glasses of wine before dinner then spill your deepest darkest bedroom secrets. Stay in control, avoid probing questions about past relationships or future plans (you aren't dating yet), and don't forget to let them talk too. Nobody likes a conversation-hogger!

5 **Stay positive.** Optimism is attractive, so glance around the bar and mention something you like, even if it's just the hand soap you've used in the loo! Don't, whatever you do, bitch about another girl's outfit or moan about the service. When you're positive, your enthusiasm will make you even more attractive.

Mum was 17 and working as a buyer for Debenhams, while Dad, who is three years her senior, was a rough-and-ready tiler.

Mum's not remotely soppy but even she says Dad fell in love with her at first sight, and who can blame him? Mum was a Jerry Hall lookalike – tall, with a long mane of curly blonde hair and big blue eyes.

Dad certainly had his work cut out with Debra Douglas. I've only ever been a one-partner woman, but Mum was courting five fellas when Dad strode onto the scene. She insists she wasn't sleeping with the others, just dating them, but all that juggling can't have been easy!

The crunch point in my parents' relationship came a couple of months after they met, when Mum moved to Italy for eight months. When her money dried up she called Dad and, presumably determined to get her back, he hopped in his Mini Cooper and drove for days across Europe to collect her. Apparently the Mini's engine blew up the moment Dad pulled into the village, but a bigger explosion followed – when Dad found out Mum was dating Giovanni, a chestnut-brown-eyed Italian barman who worked in his parents' cafe.

Fortunately, Mum saw the light. She dumped Giovanni, rode home in Dad's Mini, and by the time their ferry docked in Dover they were an item.

❀ Make up and break up (and repeat) ❀

Mum's always called the shots with men and has always had this advice for me and Georgia: 'Men should be gentlemen. No matter how much you earn, never buy a guy a drink or take him out for a meal.' I like to point out to her that we live in a modern world where equality is important, but I do agree that her rules apply for a first date!

Dad's traditional too. Although he let Georgia and me hang out with boys in our rooms, he was strictly against them sleeping over, which I considered massively embarrassing considering James was 20 when we met. But James didn't seem bothered about Dad's rule, and although it was nice to know that he loved me for me and not just for my body, after four months I began to question whether James fancied me at all.

Then came the truth: James was a virgin. One night, his best friends Martin, Pat and Big G confided in me, and revealed that James was petrified of doing it. By then I'd only done it four times myself, so I was no expert, but I was keen for our relationship to progress beyond passionate snogging into a real, adult relationship. So, one night, after sneaking him into my house after a night at Faces, I took control. And, how can I put this? We emerged victorious! Sort of . . .

The moment lasted no more than 10 seconds because Arg was rolling around on my double bed pretending to be more drunk than he actually was, slurring: 'I'm really sorry, I'm so drunk. I'm sooooo druuuuuunk!' So as first times go it was rubbish, but it did sort out James's nookie nerves, and it was so nice to see him with the weight of the world off his shoulders. Pretty soon he was in the swing of things and we were like any normal couple.

Fortunately, Mum didn't agree with Dad's sleepover rule because she could see how in love I was with James, and she turned a blind eye whenever James stayed the night. She even told fibs to Dad to keep our secret safe.

The problem, though, was James's size-10½ white Air Max, which he regularly left at our front door. Whenever Dad made the discovery as he left for work at 6 a.m. he launched the trainers in the wheelie bin. In one year James lost three pairs – all in the name of true love.

My fave 5 romantic moments

1 Mr Manolo Blahnik: James bought me a £700 pair of blue bejewelled Manolo Blahnik Hangisi heels for Valentine's Day 2012, identical to those bought by Mr Big for Carrie Bradshaw in *Sex and the City*. The store in Knightsbridge didn't have any in stock so James contacted the factory in Germany and ordered a pair to be delivered direct. I loved them so much, it was like a fashion dream come true. During the blazing row that led to our two-year break in 2012, I threw the shoes down James's driveway, and he kept them in his wardrobe for the whole time we were broken up. Then, during the *TOWIE* series 13 finale, he presented me with them. That night he hired the London Gospel Choir to sing 'our' song, Westlife's 'Flying Without Wings', which had been playing on the radio the first time I told James 'I love you' and we slow danced in my bedroom. Does it get more romantic than that?

2 Tom's trip to Paris: One busy Saturday at Bella Sorella Tom Kilbey showed up and handed me an envelope containing two tickets to Paris on the Eurostar. We'd only been dating for four months. I thought: 'We'll be in Paris just like Carrie Bradshaw and Mr Big in the penultimate episode of *Sex and the City*.' Over the long weekend we rented bikes and cycled around the city like couples do in romantic films, climbed the Eiffel Tower, walked down the Champs-Élysées and visited the Musée du Louvre, which I couldn't pronounce and called the 'Museum de Love'. Tom even got tickets for the Moulin Rouge. It was a truly romantic surprise and a memory that I treasure.

3 Our love story: For my first Christmas with James I wanted to get him something special, but I was only earning £3.25 an hour at Woolworths on the weekend so money wasn't a luxury I had. I knew James would be splashing out on me – he was raking it in working at the jeweller on Walthamstow Market – so I decided to go for a priceless gift from the heart. I bought a handmade scrapbook from a local boutique and filled it with photos of us growing up, the night we met and times we'd spent together. I worked on it for weeks and when I gave it to James he was completely blown away. To the day we broke up James said the book was his favourite ever present, which goes to show that you don't need money to be generous with your heart. One time James brought the book over, and after we broke up I never gave it back. It's something I'll one day look at to remember the good times.

4 **Mum and Dad's Mini-moon:** When Mum and Dad first started dating in 1979, American jazz singer-songwriter George Benson was huge. They both loved his music so much, and for one of their first dates Mum splashed out on two tickets to watch him live at Wembley Arena. Dad, who was still bombing around in his faithful old Mini Cooper, drove them to the venue, but on the way home his battered old motor gave up the ghost. Mum says they were so high on life after seeing their idol in concert they didn't care about being stranded. Instead, they put George Benson's album in the cassette player, turned up the song 'Love X Love' and pushed the Mini home together, laughing all the way. As for Dad, Mum says he's the least lovey-dovey man in the universe. When it comes to gifts for Mum he asks me or Georgia to buy them for him. One Christmas he took matters into his own hands and splashed out on a salt and pepper shaker set, and a couple of birthdays ago he bought her a frying pan and plastic spatula for making pancakes. Mum told him to stick the spatula up his arse.

5 **My holiday hottie:** I travelled to Thailand with my sister Georgia in December 2013. Within an hour of arriving at the legendary Full Moon Party on Koh Phangan, Georgia had disappeared for a moonlight beach snog with a south Londoner called Simon. I was fuming. I thought: 'I've brought you to the other side of the world, organised the lot, and you've ditched me for a boy on New Year's Eve!' That's when I turned to Simon's mate, Ian – he had a topknot hairstyle and a sleeve of tattoos so I thought he looked fun. 'My sister's ditched me on New Year's Eve,' I moaned. Then, summoning confidence that can only be explained by the infamous bucket cocktails, I added: 'Shall we promise to kiss at midnight?' 'Is this a joke?' laughed Ian, probably as shocked by my forwardness as my smooch-scheduling skills. When midnight came Ian tapped me on the shoulder. 'There you are,' I said. That night we didn't leave each other's sides – we went swimming in the ocean by moonlight and kissed some more under the DJ stage. We were inseparable for the whole holiday, six weeks in total. The romance was lovely while it lasted but I knew it would only ever be a holiday fling. My ability to let go stems back to constantly detaching from my foster brothers and sisters when I was a child, so nowadays, when I know something is over I rarely get upset. I just remember the good times. And Ian was good!

James will probably admit that he's always been a bit scared of Dad, and one morning in February 2008 he woke up at 5 a.m. in a panic.

'I've got to get out of here! Dave's going to find me here and freak out,' he whispered, pulling on a pair of grey tracksuit bottoms and a sweat top before creeping out of my third-floor attic room and down the stairs. That's when all hell broke loose. Or should I say all *bell* broke loose.

Riiiiiiiiiinnnnnng!

James had stupidly forgotten about the ground-floor security sensors, which set off the house alarm and automatically close the driveway gates when activated. But instead of staying put like a man to face Dad, James chose the easier option – scaling our 12-foot wrought-iron gate. I'll never forget seeing James hauling his tracksuit-clad body over the railings as Dad, his voice booming out of the upstairs window, roared: 'You bloody idiot!'

In the run-up to Christmas 2010, I had to agree with Dad on that . . .

It was around the time that Victoria Beckham had bought her husband David two miniature pot-bellied Gloucestershire Old Spot cross-breed pigs, which she nicknamed Elton and David after their mates Elton John and David Furnish. I'd mentioned this to James a few times, not because I wanted a micro pig but because I'm obsessed with animals. But James being James listened, then decided to go one better than Posh.

'I've got you a Christmas present,' he announced while we were filming the first *TOWIE* Christmas special at his parents' house. He opened the French doors to reveal a giant cage and inside was a pig, but not a micro version and not even a Babe-style piglet, but one of the oversized, pot-bellied kind.

The animal, which we named Mr Darcy, expanded daily, and was quickly shifted to Mum and Dad's perfectly manicured garden where my sister Romana's Wendy house was converted into a pigsty.

Within a matter of days, Mr Darcy had reduced the garden to a mud bath, and our West Highland terrier Trevor, who was nearing the end of his life, was being constantly terrorised.

There was only one thing for it: Mr Darcy had to go, and within two weeks of us donating him to a local farm he'd devoured a duck from a pen next to his. Trevor had been about the same size as a duck, so it had been a narrow escape for him.

🌹 Love, honour and betrayal 🌹

Mr Darcy-gate was the beginning of the end for James and me. Joining *TOWIE* had been an adjustment, not least for the boys who became overnight pin-ups to millions of girls nationwide.

Before *TOWIE*, James rarely attracted girls, but within three weeks of the show first airing the female population was Arg-obsessed. Tweets were flooding in from female admirers and wherever he went he was mobbed.

I remember in July 2011 a few of us appeared at T4 on the Beach in Weston-super-Mare in Somerset, and the whole stadium started chanting 'Arg! Arg! Arg!' which made me feel like I was dating a member of One Direction!

But inside I was scared. I'd had a fair bit of attention from the opposite sex growing up, but for Arg it was new territory and our relationship was suffering because of it. The old James would talk on the phone for hours and we had been inseparable, but the new James wasn't contacting me so often, rarely took me out and would even forget to return my calls.

Our plan had been to move in together, until James announced that he wanted us to rent a place below Mark Wright's new apartment. This infuriated me. Those two were spending so much time together and it was causing friction between James and me. I not only felt like I was playing second fiddle to Mark, but that James was pushing me away. All I wanted was our

At our favourite pie and mash shop, Robins

At the polo, the day I met James

The 298 roses Tom bought me

The scrapbook I made James when I was 16

relationship to be as strong as it had been when we first got together. Sadly, James had other ideas.

He began travelling around the country, clocking up a lot of money doing personal appearances (otherwise known as PAs) at nightclubs, where the JD-and-Cokes flowed and female attention was plentiful.

It wasn't long before I suspected that James wasn't being the faithful boyfriend he'd always been.

Note to self: when a guy becomes protective of his phone, start asking why. Around this time James's phone was glued to him at all times, set to vibrate, and he was texting more than usual. He was being secretive and I sensed that something was up, so one evening at my house when his phone buzzed I did something I'd never done before – I grabbed it, typed in his password (he'd had the same one for years) and discovered endless messages from endless girls.

James had become a sitting duck for women who pursue celebrities for one moment of passion, simply to brag about it on Twitter or, better still, make a few quid selling the details to a newspaper. James had believed these women were genuinely interested in him. What a fool. There was no question about it – we were over.

After we split, rumours began flooding Essex that Arg had cheated with someone closer to home – Amy Childs.

I needed answers from the horse's mouth – that horse being Amy – and when I confronted her on camera she admitted she had a soft spot for James but denied that anything had happened.

'You don't like it as it's another girl with Arg,' Amy told me. 'He needs a bit of flirting'. What a cheek!

It later turned out Amy had given him more than that. During our two-year break, James came clean in his autobiography and revealed that Sam Faiers had caught him snogging Amy intimately in the loos at an ITV Christmas dinner – around the same time he'd bought me Mr Darcy. He also confessed to sleeping with other girls on PAs, behaviour he excused by being 'young and foolish'.

My advice to any girl who hears cheating rumours about her boyfriend is that there's no smoke without fire, so trust your female intuition. Too many of us on *TOWIE* – Lucy Mecklenburgh and Lauren Goodger included – ignored (and didn't want to believe) the speculation. Sometimes it's hard to face up to reality and confront your fears. I didn't want to believe the telltale signs so I buried my head in the sand because I was weak and vulnerable. If you think your man is cheating, find your inner strength and get answers.

In the year that followed James and I broke up and made up 10 or more times. It played havoc with my mind and my body. I dropped a dress size and felt like I was losing the plot because we'd break up one day, be filming for *TOWIE* together a day later, start talking and be back together by the weekend. Unbeknown to me, James was copping off with other girls whenever we were on a break, including a girl called Ebru who he met in a nightclub in Romford. *Now* magazine broke that story because they got hold of some pictures of them kissing, and although James had warned me about the story (I'd been off-the-scale furious) nothing could have prepared me for my rage when I saw it in print. The entire cast were coaching it up the M1 for a *Hollyoaks* set visit in Liverpool, and it was a Tuesday, the day all the weekly magazines are published. They were doing the rounds on the coach.

The magazine reached my lap and there it was on the front page. I saw red. How could James be kissing a girl so passionately, when two days previous he was with me? I ran up the aisle of the bus waving the magazine in the air frantically. I remember ripping the pages, screaming and crying. I felt humiliated. All over again.

That's one example of the desperately unhealthy mess I was in with James.

One morning James and I woke up in bed after yet another

break up/make up episode and I felt utterly miserable. It wasn't long after a story had broken in the *Sunday Mirror* about James flirting with girls during a trip to Dubai with Mark Wright and friends, and all I could think was: 'I'm to-ing and fro-ing with a guy who is playing around with other women and I can't bear the world judging me for it.' That day at work I blanked James, which resulted in him being vile about me on camera. 'I don't know why she's arguing with me,' he said to Joey Essex. 'I had her knickers round her ankles the other night.'

> **66 UNBEKNOWN TO ME, JAMES WAS COPPING OFF WITH OTHER GIRLS WHENEVER WE WERE ON A BREAK 99**

When I watched the scene unfold on national TV I was furious and humiliated. 'How dare he talk so crudely and disrespectfully about our private life?' I thought. I picked up the phone.

'You've really pissed on your chips,' I screamed at James. 'If there was any form of hope, you've blown it. I'm not doing it anymore.'

That evening I ran round to James's clutching the Manolo Blahnik shoes he'd bought me that week and threw them down his driveway. I was adamant – we were over for good.

🌹 Taking on Tom 🌹

Shortly afterwards, Tom Kilbey walked into my life. Tom was the 6'4" younger brother of my *TOWIE* co-star and friend Cara and it was Cara who played matchmaker by giving him my number. People talk about whirlwind romances but Tom was a monsoon, and was exactly what I needed at a time when my life was falling apart. My heart didn't stand a chance.

There will come
a time when you
believe everything
is finished.
That will be
the beginning
(Louis L'Amour)

Although Tom's family is based in Loughton he lived in London's Farringdon – a cool part of the city, not far from his family's famous nightclub, Fabric, where we shared our first kiss.

With Tom in my life Essex was no longer my world. I was swanning around west London's swankiest venues, eating in glam restaurants like Hakkasan and Nobu, and partying at the coolest clubs. Within a few weeks of dating Tom even surprised me with a five-star holiday to Egypt. I was just 21 and Tom was my permanent high. I was also his first girlfriend and he idolised me. On our 298th day of dating he bought me 298 red roses, but by then I'd already fallen for him, hard.

Tom was one of the reasons I left *TOWIE* in December 2012. Dating a new guy under the watchful (and jealous) eye of James was unhealthy, and I was over my private life being devoured for public entertainment.

But within six months of leaving *TOWIE* we were over. Tom had been exactly what I needed to regain my trust in men and he reminded me how it felt to be loved. But when the honeymoon period wore off and the reality of life kicked in, so did the arguments. I started to wonder if I was ready for all that again, and if we were even compatible.

Professionally, I'd lost motivation, determination and drive. Tom was very laid back and less motivated than me and it was rubbing off. I was rocking up to Bella Sorella with scruffy hair and wearing Ugg boots – a far cry from the immaculate me of old – and Georgia wasn't happy. I wasn't pulling my weight with the shop and I wasn't there as often as I should have been given that I was no longer in *TOWIE*.

Meanwhile, my parents were concerned too. Whereas James had integrated himself into my family, Tom shunned them. Whenever he picked me up from the house he'd wait outside rather than come in for a friendly natter. Epic fail.

Mum's letter came out of the blue one Saturday morning when we were sitting in the kitchen.

'I feel like I can't talk to you about this so I've decided to write it down,' she said. 'Read it now or read it in a year but you need to know how we feel.'

Mum's an open book. She talks about everything, so to hear she felt unable to speak to me broke my heart. I had tears in my eyes before I ripped open the envelope and by the time I'd read Mum's negative feelings, there in black and white, I was in floods of tears.

Tom and I broke up in June 2013 and initially I blamed the end of the romance on my ambition and wanting to focus on my career, but let's be honest, a woman should never need to choose between her guy and her career. They should complement each other. The reason why we weren't right for each other was exactly that – we just weren't right for each other. I woke up one morning, telephoned Tom and told him it was over. I remember him crying on the phone but after that we didn't see each other again. He began dating another girl soon after. It was a clean break.

Lydia Rose of Loughton returns

After Tom, for the first time in my life no man was in the picture, so I focused 100 per cent on me. I threw myself into a pop-up tour with my clothes shop Bella Sorella, launched my first fashion collection with Lipstick Boutique, and then decided to take a leaf out of Mum's book of spontaneity and on 27 December 2013 disappeared on a seven-week trip to Malaysia, Thailand, Cambodia and Laos with Georgia. Talk about things happening at once!

In the 16 months I spent away from *TOWIE* I didn't speak to Arg because I was so furious with him. I blocked him out of my head. It was very much a case of out of sight, out of mind, but when I returned to the show in April 2014 the story changed in a heartbeat.

My break-up dos and don'ts

DO embrace Kleenex, chocolate and Ryan Gosling. Want to mourn? Then let it all out in style. Get your best mates over, crack open a family-size Galaxy and slam *The Notebook* into the DVD player. You're allowed to mope initially, so do it with those who love you and care about you but NOT alone. The same goes for drinking. Advice and hugs en masse are what's needed right now.

DON'T overdo the comfort eating. Foods high in fat, sugar and salt can actually create higher levels of the stress hormone cortisol, so nourish your body with a balanced diet. And on the subject of diets, steer clear. You might want to transform yourself into Rosie Huntington-Whiteley to show your ex what he's missing, but why punish yourself in the gym when you need love right now? Be kind to yourself.

DO socially detox. Whether it's Twitter, Facebook, Instagram, Tumblr or Vine, get the hell outta there! You won't miss the world if you beat a social media retreat for a while, and this will stop you from checking up on your ex's every move and posting cringe broken-hearted messages you'll regret. I'd also advise blocking them to avoid seeing their posts when you do finally check back into social reality.

DON'T call. If you can't bear to delete his number, rename him in your phone as 'Don't Call' or 'Stay Strong'. It'll be a good reminder not to text or call him, especially after a boozy night out.

DO remember the bad. I'm a big believer in the power of black and white, so jot down all the reasons you know your ex isn't right for you, even down to the fact that he still overcooks chicken in half a pan of vegetable oil instead of dry frying it.

DON'T date seriously too soon. By all means get out there with a hot new guy to remind yourself you are desirable and fabulous and fun, but forget getting into a new relationship too quickly. Unless you want your heart to explode like a motor in a James Bond movie.

DON'T forget why you're fabulous. Write down five reasons why you're amazing. Remember things you've achieved and mountains you've climbed in the past. It'll remind you that you can survive this . . . and you will!

My big comeback scene was in the series 11 finale at Jessica Wright and Ricky Rayment's glitzy princes and princesses fancy-dress party. The master of ceremonies introduced me as 'Princess Lydia Rose of Loughton', and as I walked into the room the reaction was insane. To the cast, it was a complete surprise. To keep my comeback a secret I had a code name, so on all the running orders I was referred to as 'Manolo'. The plan had worked. Jess and Ricky's jaws dropped to the floor. Of course, I was excited to be back with my *TOWIE* friends, but I was also anxious about coming back because lots of my friends, including Lucy Mecklenburgh, had left. I was worried that I wouldn't slot back in again. As for Arg, I'd only bumped into him once during my break – on a night out in Faces – and we'd walked straight past each other.

That night Arg, who was dressed in a bright blue *Fresh Prince of Bel-Air* outfit, scurried off only to return – after much persuasion from the producers – a few minutes later.

'How are you? Good? It's been a long time . . .' I said when we were finally face to face. I was so nervous I thought my stomach was about to drop from beneath my princess dress.

'Yeah . . . You know what? If I knew you were coming I would have gelled my hair and put on my favourite suit,' he replied.

What I hadn't anticipated was seeing Gemma Collins – who James had dated – so upset. I discovered this later when I watched the episode and saw Gemma crying on Tom Pearce's shoulder, saying: 'I think Lydia will always have that effect on him. Deep down he still loves her.'

When filming for the new series began in Marbella the execs kept James and me separate. We were booked on different flights and in separate hotels so by the time we filmed our first scene for the new series, in a restaurant, I was seriously jittery and ended up getting the giggles. Afterwards, Arg came up to me in a nightclub and said: 'You're not going with any boys tonight are you?' and I replied: 'We've just started filming together. You don't own me!' He invited me back to his hotel that night (which I declined), and that was the start of the charm offensive. After that, James was calling me a lot and was always really flirty when I saw him. I still had feelings for James, and although at first I didn't want to admit them, eventually I couldn't live a lie any longer.

But it wasn't until James and I got intimate again in October 2014 that I realised the full extent of his problems.

I knew James had been partying way too much before we broke up, but the James in front of me now was in real trouble. Physically he was bloated and slobbish but mentally he was vacant and lost. The man I'd fallen in love with, the loveable life and soul of the party, was gone.

> **66** MY BIG COMEBACK SCENE WAS IN THE SERIES 11 FINALE **99**

James was plagued with anxiety and it was terrifying to see. One month after we returned from the Marbella trip he failed to show up for a flight to Majorca where he was due to make a club appearance, and the Metropolitan Police launched a missing-persons appeal. I was in Italy on holiday and was frantic and, of course, I thought the worst. At that time I regularly did because James was vulnerable and unpredictable. He was later found asleep in a hotel room – but shortly after that he was suspended from *TOWIE*, which proved to me that he'd hit an all-time low.

TOWIE is James's ultimate love. He buzzes off it and jokes that he'll be the Ian Beale of *TOWIE* because, like the *EastEnders* character, he's been there since the beginning and will be there until the end. But he'd pushed it away and run out of chances with the show, just like he had with me.

That night I called James.

My single girl's guide to flying solo

Fresh out of a long-term relationship? Embrace singledom with these life-grabbing ideas . . .

Body talks: You want to feel and look your best so make health and fitness a top priority. Kick-start your day with a 20-minute jog, join a tennis club to meet new people or immerse yourself in the gym. Even better, sign up for a challenge like a local 10k run, beginners' triathlon or something more adventurous, to focus on an end goal. Check outcharitychallenge. com – the company that organised my cycling trips to India and across Vietnam and Cambodia. But the new you isn't all about hard slog. Book that hair appointment and treat yourself to a sumptuous massage. You're worth it!

Home sweet home: When James moved out of my home I gave the house a man-free makeover. I tidied, decluttered and cleaned every inch of the place. I made it my sanctuary by treating myself to beautiful candles and fresh flowers plus a gorgeous new sofa. Switching around the layout of the lounge also gave the place a renewed spirit.

Work it: There's never been a better time to throw yourself into your career. It'll distract you from thinking about your ex but your new lease of life, energy and space might even lead to a promotion and healthier finances. Put in the extra hours at work, investigate career-progressing courses that your company offers or take the lead on new projects to prove yourself to your boss. Heck, make that career switch you've been mulling over. Reach for the stars!

Volunteer: Not only is lending a hand a great way to meet new people, showing your support to a cause that you believe in will make you feel fulfilled, increase happiness and enhance mental wellbeing. Whether it's helping a victim of crime, walking a dog for an elderly neighbour or building a hospital garden, choose an activity that you enjoy. Visit do-it.org for ideas.

Find fulfilment: Use your time wisely and look after yourself. Partying 'til dawn might seem like fun but it won't nourish you. Instead, do things that make you happy. Throw yourself into a new hobby or activity. Yoga, cake making, learning how to fix the puncture on your mountain bike . . . whatever it is, new beginnings will leave you feeling satisfied.

Great escape: Whether it's a long weekend to a friend's house or a far-flung trip to Asia, getting away from it all is the best way to reconnect with your independent spirit. I took a three-week trip to Bali with pals, but if your friends can't drop everything why not take the plunge and go it alone? You'll find it adventurous and liberating. Another option is a singles group holiday. Contiki (0845 075 0990; contiki.com) offers 300 trips across six continents for 18 to 35s, from a New Zealand adventure to Greek island-hopping.

'I'm cutting my ties with you. You're making me ill,' I said, my voice void of emotion but tears tumbling silently down my face. It wasn't just me. James's closest friends and family felt the same and we'd agreed that we needed to stage an intervention for James to stand any chance of recovery. 'We're all cutting our ties with you, every single person around you,' I said. 'You need to get help.'

It was heartbreaking talking to James that way but he needed tough love. I knew the only way he would get better was when he lost everything, and the day he did, James left for a month's stay in rehab.

❀ Before and after The List ❀

I love Christmas. I go mad for all the traditions, shopping for gifts on Oxford Street, baking the Christmas pudding with my nan, listening to my favourite The Best Christmas Album . . . Ever CD.

But Christmas 2014 was miserable and stressful, worrying about James, who was staying put in the rehab centre, and I needed to get away. Escaping with my sister Georgia on a two-week girls' holiday to Thailand over the New Year was exactly what I needed, as was a holiday romance with a male model from Yorkshire called Ben.

Ben and I went on some dates back in England but the truth was my heart was with James, so when James emerged from rehab, I had two choices: put the past to bed and make a go of things or close the door on him and always wonder what if.

I chose the first option.

But there was a condition – I needed to know the full extent of James's past, including the cheating.

'I have to know everything,' I said one night at my house.

'I will cry and I will shout at you but I have to do this. We have to do this to move on once and for all.'

James knew he had no choice.

And so came The List – a name-by-name account of every girl he'd slept with whilst we were together.

Viewers saw this unfolding in April 2015 at the Mad Hatter's Tea Party but in reality James had handed me the list privately a few days before the fancy-dress party. *TOWIE* producers are very strict about us 'saving it for the scene', which means we're not allowed to discuss topics off camera – so that when we do talk about them, viewers get our first, honest and unrehearsed reaction and emotion. We're not actors and we can't fake how we feel, so for the most part we all adhere to this rule, but in this instance I was not about to be confronted with a list of James' conquests in front of rolling cameras and the watchful glare of the entire nation, so we agreed to meet in secret at my house.

I remember the night he handed me the list. As heartbreaking as it was, I felt relieved. James, for the first time in a long time, was being honest, and that day was our turning point. James began returning to the person I'd first fallen in love with and was showing all the signs of being back on track. He was on *TOWIE* again, in gear at the gym and back to his old self. James was the boyfriend I remembered from all those years ago.

Or so I thought.

Ten months down the line I waved goodbye to James forever. We split on Friday 25 March, a date forever stamped into my brain because that afternoon our offer on our dream future family home in east London had been accepted. It was also the day James moved out of my house for good.

It sounds sudden, and it was. I don't want to go into the ins and outs of what happened – that wouldn't be fair on James – but it became obvious that James still had problems to deal with. The more I thought about a future with James the more I suddenly

Never be afraid to tread the path alone. Know which is your path and follow it wherever it may lead you

(Eileen Caddy)

realised it wasn't what I wanted. I couldn't envisage a future with someone who was so unpredictable.

I'm glad I gave James the chance to prove himself after rehab because we had a wonderful year. We never really argued, we were house-hunting and we were best friends. I was never unhappy. But although James did change his ways he didn't change enough and, worst of all, I was beginning to hate myself for allowing him to hurt me over and over again. On the day we split I thought 'I can't be a doormat' and I knew it had to end. After seven years of making up and breaking up I knew that this time it would be for good.

The day I finished with James was one of the hardest of my life. I blocked him on my phone and all my social media and didn't speak to him for over three months until filming for *TOWIE* began again. But although it was the end of an era and incredibly emotional, I know I've made the right decision.

I don't hate James and I'll never look back on our relationship with regret because he was part of my journey, my story, my life.

This latest twist in my life hasn't sabotaged my faith in true love. I believe that the right guy will walk into my life when the time is right, but at this moment finding him isn't my priority. My main focus is me.

I've learned a lot about love from my journey with James, primarily that when I next find it I want a balanced partnership where we support each other equally.

I've been with guys in the past who have tamed me and tried to suppress me. I'm a very free spirit, I'm spontaneous, and I'm not a party animal but I like to be wild. I understand now that I need somebody who has sufficient confidence to let me be myself. I want a guy who shares my passion for life and who wants to see the world with me – and I'm ready for the journey of a lifetime.

#4
LYDIA
MEANS
BUSINESS

AMBITIOUS, INDEPENDENT AND CALM – THIS
IS HOW MY FRIENDS AND FAMILY WOULD
DESCRIBE ME IN THE WORKPLACE.

My siblings and I never had the luxury of pocket money. Firstly, because there were so many of us, but also because Mum and Dad believed in instilling a positive work ethic in us. Their favourite saying is 'Money doesn't grow on trees, you have to earn it' – and they're right.

But when opportunities come my way I always think carefully about my image. How I'm seen off screen is as important as how I'm represented on the show and is all part and parcel of the reputation I've built up as a designer and businesswoman over the years. This is my personal brand, which is all about who I am and what I want to be known for. It means making careful decisions about the opportunities that come my way.

❀ Open for business! ❀

It ended up being the Faiers sisters, Billie and Sam, who were the first cast members to own a boutique shop, Minnies in Brentwood, and soon after I was inspired to open my own. So in October 2011 I ploughed money I'd squirrelled away – £40,000 – into opening a boutique with my sister Georgia, who at the time was working as a team leader for an NHS endoscopy unit at Guy's and St Thomas' Hospital in south London.

I'd had my first experience of running my own business when I was nine years old and living on Monkham's Avenue in Woodford Green. Once a month Georgia and I set up a stall in front of our house and sold old videos and mosaic frames, which we handcrafted using broken tiles we found in Dad's van. A couple of years ago Dad confessed that he used to knock on our neighbours' doors and give them pound coins just so they would buy stuff from our stall! Bless him.

Unfortunately, the real world doesn't work like that. You can't pay customers to support your business, and if you do your business won't last long! Everything had to be right – the stock, the vibe, the location. I fell in love with the store – 251 High Road in Loughton – the moment I walked inside. The exposed brickwork and black slate floor were chic and classy. I also clocked the potential in being right beside a set of traffic lights, where people would stop in their car and glance at the window display.

One of my favourite movies of all time is the rom-com *It's Complicated*, which stars Meryl Streep and Alec Baldwin. Meryl's character is a lady who owns a successful bakery, which also sells produce and flowers. It's this approach to retail that struck a chord with me. Instead of specialising in one product we settled on selling a variety of things – flowers, cakes, kitsch homeware and unique but affordable clothing. The shop name, as suggested by Mum, would be Bella Sorella, which translates from Italian as 'beautiful sister'.

I ruled out the flower idea pretty quickly, figuring it would be too much work restocking every day. But the cupcakes had to happen. Sitting pretty in the window, they'd lure people into the store, and we ended up teaming up with a local cake shop and making £1.50 profit per cupcake. Boom!

The clothing was easy. I wanted the stock to reflect my style so I targeted all the brands I was wearing at the time – Lavish Alice, Darling, Dynasty – but our first mistake was over ordering. For the launch on 18 October 2011 I'd ordered 60 pieces of everything, so we were totally swamped! Fashion is constantly evolving and customers want to see new designs week by week, so subsequently we slashed our orders.

Our greatest
glory consists
not in never
falling,
but in rising
every time
we fall
(American proverb)

10 ways to work smart

1 **Find your passion.** As Anita Roddick, the founder of The Body Shop, once said: 'To succeed you have to believe in something with such a passion that it becomes a reality.' Whether you're in school, in college or already out there working, ask yourself: 'What do I enjoy, believe in and trust?' You'll be spending a lot of time in the company of your career so you need to be friends with it. If you're not happy with what you're doing don't be afraid to try something new and go after your dream.

2 **Don't compare yourself.** When I started out in *TOWIE* it was easy to get caught up in what the other girls were doing. It would have been easy to fret about whether they were being booked for more photoshoots than me, or if my red-carpet dress wasn't rated as highly by a magazine as theirs. If you find yourself measuring yourself against your peers – stop! Learn to acknowledge another person's success without putting yourself down. Your story is your story, theirs is theirs. End of.

3 **Be organised.** If a messy house is a messy mind, the same goes for your desk space. Organisation, structure and time management are the key to being productive and happy, and it shows others you're in order. I sort all my paperwork into relevant folders and store them in a filing cabinet, and I'm obsessive about keeping a diary on my iPhone. Also, to-do lists are great, especially if you guesstimate the length of each task. It'll help you be realistic about how much you can fit into a day!

4 **Sod 'sometime'.** How often do you say 'Let's get together sometime' or 'I'll do that sometime soon'? Forget being vague and start being specific. If a job takes less than two minutes, do it immediately; if you're discussing meeting a friend or colleague, get your diary out and plan it. Life's too short for 'sometime'.

5 **Focus, focus, focus.** Disable alerts on your phone. You'll be amazed at how much more you can get done when you're not checking your phone every 10 seconds.

6 **Ask for advice.** When I launched Bella Sorella, Sam and Billie Faiers could easily have thought: 'We're not sharing our business secrets with Lydia – she's competition.' Instead, they've been very helpful whenever I've gone to them asking for advice. Once you're a guru yourself, don't forget to pay the favour forward. Treat others like you would like to be treated and karma will come back to reward you.

7 **Don't be a dweller.** If you've had a bad day, don't spend hours thinking about it afterwards. I've heard that replaying conversations or events heightens stress to the same levels as when they actually happened. Instead, take a few minutes to think about it, then visualise yourself closing the door on whatever is bothering you. Go to the cinema, see a friend or listen to some music to distract yourself completely.

8 **Don't mix business with pleasure.** While it's good to have solid, fruitful relationships with contacts and employees, business is business. I have great relationships with the clothing brands that I stock in Bella Sorella, but our agreements are written into a legal contract.

9 **Face your finances.** I have a spreadsheet to keep track of my earnings and expenses. If you're self-employed, never forget to squirrel away 20 per cent or more of everything you earn to cover your annual tax bill. When I joined *TOWIE* I had no clue that being self-employed meant I had to do a self-assessment tax return, so I got an eye-watering tax bill after 18 months! I almost had a nervous breakdown. It was just as I bought my first house, shortly after leaving *TOWIE*. Luckily they let me pay it back in instalments, but it was a massive lesson.

10 **Work, rest and play.** Being a hard worker, being dedicated and believing in yourself are essential to doing well at any stage of your life. But it's important to take care of yourself, too. No successful people operate on no sleep and a diet of junk. Exercise, take regular breaks and eat good food. It will keep you healthy and contribute to a positive attitude, good motivation and happy relationships. Finally, remember to smile. It tricks your body into feeling more positive.

If an item sold well we reordered. If it didn't we learned the hard way. Initially, Georgia and I weren't very good businesswomen. We were too afraid to ask suppliers for a deal, but now I'm good at bartering in business. It's amazing how quickly you learn on the job!

We didn't realise how big Bella Sorella was going to be. From the launch day it was mayhem and at weekends our feet never touched the ground. Queues trailed down the high street and we had so many customers that sometimes we had Dad step in as a bouncer! We were selling 300 cupcakes every Saturday and were bringing in so much *TOWIE* tourism to Loughton that managers of other shops began thanking us for saving their businesses! We had customers to the store travelling from as far away as America and Australia.

Popping up everywhere!

Bella Sorella was booming for the first two years, largely thanks to our regular visits from *TOWIE* fans. But after 24 months in business our in-store profits were down – largely because of competition from the huge Westfield shopping mall in nearby Stratford – so it was time for action.

My motto in business is 'If it's not working, change it!' There's no point burying your head in the sand and praying for a miracle. Business is all about evolution. Nothing stays the same so you have to be flexible and open to new ideas.

'We need to find a way to generate the buzz we had when we launched,' I announced to Georgia one Saturday afternoon in the shop over a hot cup of tea. 'How can we reach out to *TOWIE* fans who just want to buy a Bella Sorella cake and candle?'

'We need to take Bella Sorella *to* the *TOWIE* fans,' replied Georgia. 'We need to go to the shopping malls, spread the word about our products and promote the website.' And right there, our pop-up shop tour plans were born.

I had to get my game on. I hit Google and found the contact details for PR managers at shopping malls where celebrities had been booked to turn on the Christmas lights – malls that understood the power of celebrity. Within a few weeks we had secured week-long spaces at eight shopping centres across the UK for no cost. All I'd have to do was give some interviews to the press and a few fashion bloggers at each location. It was win-win for Bella Sorella – store space *and* publicity.

❝ I HAD TO GET MY GAME ON ❞

I wanted to give away prizes galore in every town, incentives for people who registered to receive our fashion newsletter (email addresses mean access to potential customers). Sourcing prizes became a favour trade-off. I agreed with spa and beauty product companies to do appearances at their events in exchange for their products and experiences.

The tour kicked off in July 2013 on Carnaby Street in London, and some of my friends, including Denise van Outen, Zoe Hardman and a few of the *TOWIE* girls like Lucy Mecklenburgh, came out to support me.

Once the glamour of the press call was over the hard work began. Georgia and I hit the road in our white van with our three assistants. The first stop was Bristol, and over nine weeks we covered nine towns, including Southampton, Sheffield, Liverpool and Glasgow. I was the only named driver on the van, which meant I was in the driver's seat for a lot of miles!

It was a hard slog but so rewarding. Every place we turned up at the reaction was insane, and the further we travelled the crazier the reception we got. The people in Scotland were off the scale!

So what's the future for Bella Sorella? In September 2016 we closed the doors of the boutique and transferred our entire business online. The shop was brilliantly successful while it lasted but, sadly, with the demise of the local high street and the massive competition of a major shopping mall it made sense to focus all our energy and investment on our ever-growing online presence.

In the weeks before we closed up, people were asking me 'Will you be sad not to have a store anymore?' and my answer was always no, because our website is off the charts. We ship to lots of countries including Canada and Spain so the world is, literally, our oyster. The shop was incredible, but you can't be emotional about business. Change equals profit and we're constantly evolving.

❀ blog: noun ❀

1. a regularly updated website or web page, typically one run by an individual or small group, that is written in an informal or conversational style.

As I'm sure you've now realised, fashion is one of my biggest joys and is the reason I launched my blog in 2012. I kept getting asked via Twitter for details of outfits I'd worn, but I became increasingly frustrated with the 140-character limitation because I couldn't always fit in website links to items I was wearing. Plus, I've always loved writing. I decided a blog would be the best place for me to showcase my style and write about the clothes and beauty products I love in more detail.

Why blog? It comes down to passion. When you love anything, be it make-up, food or music, you probably feel you have so many ideas, opinions and comments to make about the topic – which is how I felt about fashion. You might start a blog to share those ideas, or because you love writing and want to have a creative outlet to pour yourself into.

9 tips for blogging the Bright way

1 Content: What are you going to blog about? What makes you different to all the other bloggers out there? Start with a catchy name and a clear concept and build it from there.

2 Quality: It sounds obvious, but only post good content. If it's not good your followers won't return for more. Forget brain dumping in five minutes and hitting publish. If a good post requires two days of effort, allow two days. One fabulous bit of content is better than three mediocre pieces. There are hundreds of blogs out there and many are rubbish, so make yours amazing.

3 Picture it: Your blog isn't just about words; the visuals have to scream off the page. I invested in a Canon 600D camera to take cool, edgy shots of myself wearing the clothes in beautiful locations, and I do a new shoot every couple of weeks and get friends and family members to take the pictures.

4 Sharing is caring: The more you big up other bloggers by sharing their content the more likely they are to support you. These people are called influencers.

5 Be social media savvy: Promote your blog using Twitter, Instagram and Facebook. The more you spread across all platforms the wider your reach will be.

6 Interact: When you get comments on your blog, respond. Comments are a measure of engagement, and the more you interact with people reading your content the more invested they will be in what you have to say. Creating a mailing list is a savvy way of keeping your followers informed about new posts, reminding them to revisit your blog and letting them know about your new business if and when you start it!

7 Shhhhh!: Many people check out blogs at work and won't appreciate Beyoncé blasting out of their computer when their boss is approaching to explain next month's targets. Avoid background music.

8 Invest time: I'll make no bones about it . . . running a blog eats into your day like a caterpillar munching through a lettuce leaf, but a good blog requires dedication. I blog once a week and devote four full days a month to pulling it together, plus two days for photoshoots.

9 Consistency: Choose the same day every week to post a blog update so your followers know when to expect new material.

If you're running a business, in an internet-obsessed society it's also a way of creating an online presence – which is key if you want to be taken seriously in your field. Blogs show people, instead of just telling them, that you're passionate about what you do and prove that you're good at it. It's also a way of expanding that personal brand I mentioned earlier and it proves to people that you are what it says on the tin.

If you run a business, the key to making your blog an asset is linking it to your website. The more often you post content, the more visitors you'll get to your website. Your blog will eventually become a promotional tool for your product or service, and my blog has definitely helped drive business to the Bella Sorella website, which we launched six months after the shop. I don't make a massive income from it but it's always been a passion project for me. I love inspecting the clothes when they arrive, wearing them for the first time, taking the pictures and seeing the results and comments on my blog.

My first fashion collection is born

Lauren Conrad has long been a career idol of mine, and she's similar to me because she found fame on one of the first reality television shows, *Laguna Beach*. Okay, she's not very similar to me because she's a multi-millionaire and lives in LA! But she started out on a reality show and was one of the first to benefit from the popularity of reality television in the early 2000s. In time, she managed to build a successful brand and career, using *The Hills* –the programme she was in after *Laguna Beach* – as a platform, and has credited her fame with helping her promote her business and getting her introductions to the right people. She's also been quite outspoken about struggling to be taken seriously in the fashion industry when you start out in entertainment.

If you're a celebrity and you find the right companies to back you, you can launch anything, so a lot of reality stars bleed the market dry by putting their face to every product under the sun. I believe that if you do this nobody trusts that you're genuinely invested in what you're selling. How can one person know how to formulate a fake tan, create a perfume and design clothes?

Early on I was approached by a well-known fake tan brand to launch my own range, which made no sense at all. I had the palest skin of all the girls on *TOWIE* – it's down to my Irish heritage – so I made it clear that I didn't want to be the type of celebrity who puts my name to everything, especially products I didn't have a clue about.

> **❝ I DIDN'T WANT TO BE THE TYPE OF CELEBRITY WHO PUTS MY NAME TO EVERYTHING ❞**

My manager Kirsty secured me a meeting with Lipstick Boutique, a north London-based company that specialises in celebrity fashion and has sold collections by reality stars like Jessica Wright and Rosie Fortescue from *Made in Chelsea*.

I'd already identified a niche in the market. When I was buying stock for Bella Sorella I couldn't find a brand that was vintage-inspired but also commercial. I had an idea to make feminine, vintage-style clothing accessible to girls who shopped on the high street.

At the Lipstick Boutique meeting I laid my cards on the table.

'I want to be very hands-on, I want total control of the collection, I want to hold my own buyer meetings, I want it to be totally me,' I said, determined not to put my name to a cookie-cutter celebrity collection, identical to all the others. I felt confident. I knew about fashion, I was clued up about the buying process, and the team seemed to believe in me.

I signed a deal with Lipstick Boutique and eventually it made me enough to put down a deposit on a house. I'd promised

Lipstick Boutique the world, insisting that my collection would be the first to make it into high street shops where I already had contacts.

I proved them right. Soon after my collections launched big buyers like Very.co.uk and New Look were on board, and they reported huge sales. I was over the moon.

Following the success of the first collection, a 10-dress Christmas capsule, I sketched more designs and five more collections followed for spring/summer and autumn/winter, incorporating separates, daywear and eveningwear. I was hands-on from the off, at the factory in Tottenham, north London, making mood boards and working with a fabulous designer called Androulla Stylianou who gave life to my ideas with her amazing sketches. I visited the London Fabric Show to pick out swatches and followed the design process from start to finish.

At my press days I sat with journalists and took them through the design process. I showed them the Marilyn Monroe dress with an organza bow that I loved, and then I unveiled my interpretation of it. My frock had a shortened hem, I swapped organza for the softer chiffon, and I lowered the V-neckline. The journalists could see the evolution and could tell I wasn't just another celebrity putting my face to a product.

My enthusiasm and input worked. I was the first celebrity brand to get a collection on internet shopping site ASOS (which many people struggle to pronounce – it's Ace-oss, by the way!).

Getting ASOS to meet me was anything but easy. I'd approached them more times than the fingers on both hands, and each time they'd said no because they were dead against featuring collections by celebrities.

Somehow Kirsty got me an in at ASOS HQ and I knew I had one chance to convince them that my clothes would make them money.

In January 2014 my dream came true. The Lydia Rose Bright collection was up on ASOS and within three months it was the third best-selling brand on the site. The same month River Island bought the collection, at the same time as Rihanna's second collection dropped, and I kept thinking: 'Oh my God, my collection is up there alongside Rihanna's!' It was insane.

I truly thought: 'Fashion is my calling.' I was living and breathing it, creativity was pouring out of me. I even went to an open day at the London College of Fashion to investigate taking a part-time BA (Hons) degree in fashion design. Forget *TOWIE* – I was going to be a fashion designer! In the end, the course was too time-consuming, so I stuck with what I was doing so well – producing fashion collections with an amazing team.

The Lydia Rose Bright collection lasted for five seasons and I'm now in talks with a major online retailer about launching a brand-new range. So, true to Walt Disney's words (--->), I'm still dreaming and will always be dreaming about fashion.

If you can dream it, you can do it

(Walt Disney)

#5
STYLE TIPS AND RED LIPS

IN MY EYES, ONLY A FEW WOMEN QUALIFY TO GO DOWN IN HISTORY AS THE BEST DRESSED OF ALL TIME: BRIGITTE BARDOT, GRACE KELLY, AUDREY HEPBURN AND MARILYN MONROE.

In my house I've got shelves of books devoted to 1950s style, and if I could jump into Doctor Who's TARDIS right now I'd pop back to that era, knock on Marilyn's front door and ask for a nose around her closet.

I've got Mum to thank for nurturing my independent fashion spirit and inspiring me to not follow trends just for the sake of it.

Mum has never been like other Essex mums. She's not into fake tans and fancy blow-dries. Her skin is pale, her hair is wild and natural and the same can be said for her fashion individuality. But growing up, Mum's uniqueness was a regular source of embarrassment for me.

Mum's been friends for years with Nicky Blackwell, the mother of my *TOWIE* co-star Liam Blackwell. She's also Liam's godmother. Nicky was born in Kartarpur in Punjab, Pakistan, and has the most beautiful collection of saris in gorgeously bright colours. One year, she had a closet clear-out, and Mum went along for a rummage, returning home hours later with bags of Nicky's saris and kaftans. Overnight, Mum's eastern phase was born.

'Why is your mum wearing clothes like my mum?' asked one Indian kid at home-time, as we approached the school gate where Mum was chatting, a vision in bright purple, green and gold, oblivious to my embarrassment.

'Oh, she's just eccentric,' I replied. 'Eccentric' was a word I'd heard Mum use once before to describe her style, and she wasn't wrong.

Most afternoons that summer term I'd hear a *dingle-ing, dingle-ing* sound wafting through the classroom window, and it was Mum coming to pick me up, wearing her favourite sari teamed with jingling-bell Indian slippers called *khussa*. Mum's bright red Swedish wooden clogs were equally humiliating. Not only did they resemble strawberry-coloured horse hooves, but they sounded like them too. I could hear her clip-clopping towards the school gate from a mile off. These days, I'm so grateful that Mum wasn't an M&S mum and that she experiments with her style choices. It's not surprising either, given she's lived and breathed fashion her entire life.

> ❝ MUM'S LIVED AND BREATHED FASHION HER ENTIRE LIFE ❞

In 1979, after a year working for Debenhams as a fashion buyer, Mum was recruited by a huge fashion business run by American socialite Gloria Vanderbilt, who was a household name in the 1970s because of her signature fashion jeans. As personal assistant to company director Goggie Troughton – a tall and skinny powerhouse from Sweden, who had balls of steel and a gold Amex card to match, and a touch of Cruella De Vil about her – Mum lived the fashion high life. For five years under Goggie's wing, she worked on catwalk shows in the West End, was in charge of casting all the models, and travelled to places like Germany, Spain and Ireland.

But it was my Nanny Maureen's sister Doris, affectionately called Nanny Doll, who was our family's true fashion leader. In the late 1950s Nanny Doll was appointed director of a fashion house called Pierre Elegante, where she worked until she was 65. The company made jackets and skirts for M&S, and Doris travelled the world – flying to Milan one day then Paris the next, and rubbing shoulders with the coolest names. She's godmother to the only son of legendary Fleet Street journalist Jean Rook, and always socialised with models and celebrities.

My dear Nanny Doll is now in her late 80s, and although she still has the mind of an 18-year-old, her body is slowly deteriorating. She now lives in a sleepy Essex village called Kelvedon Hatch – a marked contrast to the days she resided in a penthouse apartment in the West End's Conduit Street! Whenever I drop in to see her she says: 'If I pop off tomorrow, I've lived a fabulous life.' I can't quibble. I'm so proud of her achievements in the fashion world and I hope she's proud of mine.

❀ Wear for art thou? ❀

By the time I hit my early teens I was seriously getting into fashion. One of my first trend obsessions was the classic combo of pink Juicy Couture velour tracksuit and Ugg boots, closely followed by another corker: Timberland boots, jungle trousers (made from ripstop cotton) and a white string vest. I was the unofficial fifth member of Louise Redknapp's band Eternal!

It wasn't until I was a sixth-former and no longer required to wear a uniform, that my own unique sense of style began to emerge. This stage in my life coincided with an infatuation with my ultimate style and life icon: *Sex and the City* protagonist Carrie Bradshaw, played by the beautiful Sarah Jessica Parker. Carrie had it all – a walk-in wardrobe stuffed full of glamorous clothes, a dream life in New York working as a writer (this mirrored my own ambition to be a fashion journalist), her own income, and endless dates with gorgeous men to fabulous events like the ballet, art exhibitions and classical music concerts.

How to get the Lydia look

Pastels: Tinkerbell was my fashion icon when I was five, and I still dress like a young girl who never grew up! Girlie pastels are a huge staple in my wardrobe and I wear them during summer and winter. Miss Selfridge is full of pastels and grown-up fairy-princess dresses.

Heels: I've got over 100 pairs of shoes and 99 per cent of them are heels, because flats don't excite me. I'm a big fan of the timeless court heel. I love wearing lace and embellishment, so courts prevent me from looking OTT. They're also brilliantly leg-slimming. Dune does a great classic court all year round, and New Look is also a fabulous choice if you're on a budget.

Hats: I've never been great at doing my own hair, so hats are my saviour. A hat can make any outfit look cool and edgy. Stick on a pair of jeans, a comfy knit and pumps, then throw on a trilby and *voilà*! You've got a statement outfit. I own at least 25 hats. A straw summer hat is a must for holiday season (head to New Look for a steal) while M&S is great for winter hats.

Dresses: Dresses make up 60 per cent of my wardrobe and are the key to dressing elegantly. My favourite styles are skater and tulip, which cinch in the waist and skim the hips and bum, creating the illusion of curves and covering the tummy (my least favourite body part). If you're a pear or hourglass figure, though, a fitted bodycon style is a more flattering choice.

Shoulder flashing: My legs are my best asset but I'm a believer in 'less is more', so I don't like showing too much flesh. A sexy and demure alternative to revealing your legs or cleavage is to show off your shoulders, which is what women did in the 1950s. Virgos Lounge is a fabulous brand that does lots of gorgeous off-the-shoulder embellished party dresses. Find them on ASOS.

Carrie also had an awesome group of friends – Charlotte, Miranda and Samantha – and like millions of girls around the globe my friends and I rechristened ourselves according to the personality we best matched. Needless to say, I was *always* Carrie!

In those days, I dreamed of being a City girl in London and working in a high-flying job, so my sixth-form look screamed Carrie Bradshaw chic – pointed patent court heels, pencil skirt, black tights and a white fitted shirt.Then there was the hair. I've inherited a naturally curly mane from my mum, which I used to GHD to within an inch of its life when straight hair *à la* Rachel from *Friends* was all the rage. But as soon as I hit sixth form, when my inner Carrie taught me to embrace the curl, VO5 styling mousse and scrunching were my thing.

My look went down a storm with the other girls at school. They'd tell me I was 'so glamorous', a compliment I loved, and, needless to say, the reaction to my mature new image filled me with confidence. At 16 we all want to be grown up, so isn't it ironic that in our mid-20s and 30s we'd do anything to rewind to the days of no responsibilities?

My passion for vintage emerged just before I joined *TOWIE* at the age of 18, when I was working in the quirky north London area of Camden, where everyone embraces their individuality. It's also a great place to shop for unusual vintage items. Every lunch break I'd dash out to the Stables Market and spend the hour rummaging through the wardrobes of past generations in the many vintage stalls. I was equally obsessed with the vintage warehouse Beyond Retro on Cheshire Street, in east London's Shoreditch. A vintage warehouse is like an Aladdin's cave of yesteryear's fashion. Buyers source from boot sales, bespoke charity shops and vintage markets. Most of these are in the big cities, and are untapped goldmines. Independent traders trawl the country's vintage or antique markets for their stock.

But although I loved my style it wasn't in keeping with the

looks that my friends were rocking at the time. I remember going to Club 195 in Epping wearing one of the first vintage outfits I bought, from Beyond Retro – a pink long-sleeved flower-print dress, which I wore with a tulle underskirt. I loved the look. Unfortunately, my taste didn't sit pretty with a rather bitchy local girl, who sauntered over to me with a glass of white wine and a seriously bad attitude.

'Why have you come out wearing your grandma's curtains?' she smirked, looking me up and down. I was so shocked I didn't say anything, but my friends stepped in and told her what for.

I'd left the house feeling amazing about wearing my beautiful vintage dress for the first time, but in two seconds flat Jordan's comment had floored me. Insecurity washed over me like a tidal wave and I instantly wanted to be anywhere but 195, so within an hour I was home and tearing off the dress. As I climbed into bed with tears in my eyes I vowed never to wear vintage again.

But the next day I woke up defiant.

'My dress did look like my grandma's curtains,' I thought. 'But I'd choose my grandma's curtains over a boring black bodycon dress any day of the week!'

I've never turned my back on vintage since.

🌹 There's no business like Frow business 🌹

Fashion truly feeds my soul and I buzz off it. During London Fashion Week I'm locked into fashion website Style.com to keep tabs on what my favourite designers are showing on the catwalks.

I've been fortunate to attend a few London Fashion Week shows in the past. I sat front row at the show of London designer fashion brand PPQ in September 2011 and February 2012, and have been to many Fashion Scout and Fashion Fringe shows, which showcase up-and-coming designers.

Closet confidential

We all have clothes that make us remember special moments. These are the pieces in my wardrobe that I love the most, because they stir up my fondest memories . . .

1 **Sunflower dress:** Mum bought this dress in her 20s. She fell in love with it because the region around Porto Recanati in Italy, where Mum holidayed as a child, is famous for its sunflowers. Mum loaned this to me when I appeared on stage at T4 on the Beach in July 2011. I'm more of a glamorous dresser and not one to wear Daisy Dukes and wellies at festivals, so this dress saved the day!

2 **Cowboy hat:** After trekking up Machu Picchu in Peru in 2015 in aid of CoppaFeel!, the breast-cancer-awareness charity, we ended up in a city called Cusco, where I bought this leather cowboy hat. I promised myself that I'd wear it with pride on my next holiday, but I've yet to take the plunge. But the hat is a reminder of that epic charity challenge, and for that reason it'll always sit proudly in my wardrobe.

3 **Vintage cape:** I inherited this 100 per cent wool cape from my mum and wore it on my first ever appearance on *TOWIE*. It was autumn and I'd just returned from Marbs so most of my wardrobe was summery. I had no money to shop for a cool outfit so Mum came to the rescue again! She lent me her cape and I wore it over a cream dress with thick black tights and shoe boots. I love the outfit because it was unique and I felt like Mum had given her seal of approval, which gave me a bit of confidence during that f irst nerve-wracking scene.

4 **Sea Folly swimsuit:** I bought this in Australia while filming *I'm A Celebrity . . . Get Me Out Of Here! NOW!* and it became my uniform while filming *Celebrity Island with Bear Grylls* for Channel 4. My double-padded M&S bra ended up being used as a makeshift water filter, so this swimsuit was the only undergarment I wore for two weeks. When I left the show I left the cossie behind because it was stained, full of holes and stank to high heaven, but when I got home I bought a replacement. One glance at it makes me feel so proud of my achievements.

5 **Green handbag:** My Nanny Maureen's other sister Joan passed away shortly after her son, about 20 years ago. Apparently she died of a broken heart. Her green snakeskin leather handbag eventually found its way to me, and I wore it for the first time at the *TV Choice* Awards in March 2013. I felt honoured to own such a beautiful item and truly feel that Auntie Joan was there with me in spirit.

6 My first shoes: Mum kept hold of all her kids' first shoes and mine are a pair from John Lewis. They look like clumpy clown shoes and are hideous compared to the ones she bought my siblings, but I love the fact that I now own over 100 pairs of shoes and that these were my first pair. History in the making!

7 Rodrigo Otazu necklace: I loved everything that Carrie Bradshaw wore in the movie *Sex and the City 2*, especially this necklace. When I attended a launch party for the DVD at Swarovski on Regent Street in April 2011 I nearly choked on my glass of champagne – because there it was for sale! At £300 it was way out of my price range, so imagine my delight when James presented it to me in the car on the way home. He'd secretly bought it and I was so happy I screamed! I've worn it loads since. It's the perfect accessory to a simple black dress.

8 BAFTAs 2011 dress: Gifting is one of the best celebrity perks. It's when a brand lends or gives you a product, knowing that when members of the public see you with it, their sales will go up. The ballgown that I wore to the BAFTAs in 2011 was the first thing I had ever been gifted, and it catapulted me into magazine 'best dressed' lists for the very first time. Ahead of the event I had no money to buy a ballgown so Mum, who had a friend at a fashion brand called Dynasty, arranged for me to visit their showroom in Borehamwood. It was fashion heaven – rail upon rail of dresses, and I spent hours wading through them, trying on at least fifty before I settled on a gorgeous silver tulle flower appliqué number. All the *TOWIE* girls rocked up in metallic – what a fluke! I've never worn the dress since, but I'll never get rid of it because it's the dress that made me realise that I wanted to be appreciated for my fashion. Dynasty later renamed this dress The Lydia and it was a sell-out!

9 Chanel monochrome heels: Shortly after I bought my first house in December 2012 I took my then boyfriend Tom Kilbey to New York. Walking down Fifth Avenue I announced: 'I just want to be Carrie Bradshaw for the day,' which was code for 'I want to spend lots of money in designer stores.' But I couldn't afford to. I'd thrown all my savings into my mortgage and had £1,000 left to buy a fridge and other household items. When I saw these shoes in Chanel, all sense went out the window. 'They're very Carrie Bradshaw!' I said to the sales assistant, who replied: 'Carrie would *love* these.' I was sold, even though they'd been imported from France and cost £800 – £200 more than they would have cost in the UK! I used my new fridge fund to pay for them, so was fridgeless for the next three months. Carrie used her oven for storage though, so I wasn't bothered that I was minus a fridge. I had fabulous footwear!

10 Gold clutch: I spotted this ornate hard gold metal clutch on a market stall in Delhi during a cycling challenge to India with my friend Denise van Outen in April 2012. Denise is a big fan of toot – knick-knacks you buy on holiday that you don't really need – and I now use this bag all the time. I broke the metal strap when I took it to Las Vegas in June 2016, so I now use it as a box clutch.

One dream I'd like to make happen before my 30th birthday (I have a 30 before 30 list – check out the penultimate chapter) is to attend a top designer runway show at London Fashion Week, and I'm not even fussed about being Frow. A back-row seat at Burberry would be just as fabulous!

Although I have an obsession with designer catwalk shows and am lucky enough to own a few pairs of designer shoes, I've only worn designer outfits a handful of times – the first time being in September 2015 at the UK premiere of Anne Hathaway's movie *The Intern.* That evening I wore a vintage tweed Chanel coat and matching Chanel dress, which I'd bought four months earlier from a lady in Essex who scours shops for vintage pieces and sells them on to girls like me. I paid £800 for the outfit, which sounds expensive, but Chanel holds its value so I justified it by thinking: 'Even if I only wear it once and sell it I'll make my money back.' But I have no intention of doing that!

It was a very special night. I'd been approached by Universal Pictures to front a competition at the permiere, and given that two of my favourite actors were going to be on the red carpet – Anne and Robert De Niro – a super-expensive outfit was a must!

❀ Cosmetic ordering ❀

As a little girl I would constantly say to Mum: 'I can't wait until I'm older so I can wear make-up, chew gum and drink Diet Coke'. I was obsessed with becoming an adult, and all those things were out of the question until, as my parents often said, 'you're older'.

I turned 'older' on my 13th birthday. It was the day that Mum gave me permission to buy my first items of make-up. I raced to Boots before the candles had even cooled on my birthday cake, to purchase a Nivea tinted lip balm and a blue Rimmel eyeliner, which I wore on the water line like all the other girls at school.

How to shop smart for vintage

Hunt wisely. On the whole, charity vintage shopping is hit and miss. Usually, you'll be hard pushed to find anything older than an M&S jumper circa 2006, but if you travel out of the cities and head for villages and towns that have large wealthy retired communities, you might bag some age-old designer gems.

Take your time. You can't race around a vintage store in 15 minutes. Stock usually isn't size-ordered or colour-coordinated, so allow at least two hours to do the place justice.

Don't be afraid to inspect. Take the items off the rail, inspect stitching, and feel it with your hands. It might stink because the clothes aren't always washed, so be prepared to dry clean everything you buy.

Use your imagination. If you find an item that you love but it's too big, think 'seamstress'. I've bought clothes that were around a size 14 and had them taken in to fit me. Vintage shopping is about thinking outside the measurement box.

Try before you buy. I'm a fan of double-breasted coats, little tuxedo dresses, polka dots, frills and full skirts, so I'm always on the hunt for these items because they particularly suit my body shape. You'll only learn what suits you by trying things on.

Look smart. Keep your eyes peeled for fabrics that were more common in clothing from yesteryear. Don't end up buying something that's actually a noughties rip-off. You don't find scrunched-up shiny organza on the high street nowadays, for example. Past generations also wore super-thick wool blends (the old-fashioned answer to scuba), which is less commonplace now. Also keep an eye out for zips – until the 1960s they used only metal or aluminium zips, throughout the 1960s it was nylon, then plastic took over. Finally, look at the labels – washing care instructions weren't compulsory in the UK and America until the 1970s, and if the label says 'Made in China', it's not vintage!

Should you ever stumble upon one of my early *TOWIE* episodes you'll rightly argue that make-up wasn't my forte. I didn't have a clue what I was doing. In fact, 'contouring' was a word I would have associated with my dad's tiling company, not my cheekbones!

Thanks to *TOWIE* I've been given the ultimate privilege – one-to-one sessions with some of the industry's most incredible and experienced make-up artists. And over the years I've fortunately learned some amazing make-up techniques from the best in the business.

Lyndsey Harrison is the one make-up artist I credit for rescuing me from cosmetics car crash. We met in December 2011, shortly after I joined *TOWIE*, when she was also starting out. She reached out to me and some of the other *TOWIE* girls via Twitter and offered her services for free. It's been an incredible journey for both of us, and now Lyndsey is responsible for glamming up everyone from Denise van Outen to Nadine Coyle. I count Lyndsey as one of my nearest and dearest. She has the warmest heart and is incredibly talented, and deserves all of her success.

She 'got' my look from the start. She'd always say 'Let's try a flick eye' or 'Let's throw in a little vintage curl.' Over the next few pages, Lyndsey's going to give you her step-by-step guides to recreating my three signature make-up looks.

But before we get to the routines, let's talk about the tools . . .

❁ Tools of the trade ❁

Lots of people don't use brushes when applying make-up, but I've been very lucky to watch professionals at work (on me!) and the difference a good brush can make is amazing.

Brushes range in price from affordable to investment buys, so my advice is to build your collection up slowly and to think about which brushes you're going to use the most.

Below are the brushes that Lyndsey uses the most for my signature looks.

✴ FOUNDATION AND CONCEALER

Real Techniques Buffing Brush – good for blending in foundation and creating an airbrushed look without fingerprints.
Real Techniques Miracle Complexion Sponge – the edge allows you to get right up to the lash line, around the nose and up to the corner of your eye.
Real Techniques Pointed Foundation Brush – great for applying foundation and also concealer.

✴ POWDER AND HIGHLIGHTER

MAC 150 Large Powder Brush – a full, dense brush that achieves good coverage.
MAC 224 Tapered Blending Brush – a light and feathery brush that works well with both powder and highlighter.

✴ CONTOURING

Cassie Lomas 'Polly' Angled Brush – this is a soft brush that allows you to build the shade evenly.
MAC 184 Fan Brush – good for application at the hairline and forehead, and good for contouring (with powder) around the cheekbones and sides of the nose.
Real Techniques Setting Brush – good application for cheeks.

✗ BROWS

Real Techniques 202 Angled Liner – a tiny brush for natural application of powder or cream.

MAC 263 Small Angle Brush – a slanted brush for firm application of colour.

✗ EYESHADOW

Crown C124 Firm Shadow – a small, soft brush. Good for applying full colour to lid.

Crown C139 Stiff Tapered Crease – good for contouring on lid.

MAC 217 Blending Brush – any kind of eye shading needs a soft brush, and this is brilliant at blending colours and softening the line in the socket.

Crown C433 Pro Blending Fluff Brush – similar to the Mac 217, but one that won't break the bank.

MAC 219 Pencil Brush – good for applying highlighter to the tear duct.

Sigma E30 Pencil Brush – good for taking eyeshadow under the eye.

Morphe M431 Precision Pencil Crease Brush – a good, cheaper alternative to the Sigma E30 Pencil Brush.

✗ EYELINER

MAC's Eyeliner Brush 210 – you need a dense yet fine brush to apply steady, smooth lines and this is perfect for that.

Fierce Face M65 Small Eyeliner Brush – a really good value brush for achieving steady lines and flicks.

LOOK 1

HOLLYWOOD WAVE WITH CLASSIC RED LIP AND FLICK

This look is great for a winter red-carpet event when you're wearing dark colours, because the colour of the lip really pops. Below are the products Lyndsey and I use.

SHOPPING LIST

FACE

☐ **Moisturisers:** Nars Luminous Moisture Cream and Bobbi Brown Hydrating Eye Cream

☐ **Primer:** MAC Prep + Prime Skin

☐ **Correctors and concealers:** BECCA Backlight Targeted Colour Corrector in Pistachio and MAC Pro Longwear Concealer in NC15

☐ **'Fixer':** MAC Studio Fix fluid in NC30

☐ **Powder:** Bobbi Brown Sheer Finish Loose Powder in Pale Yellow

☐ **Contouring:** Anastasia Beverly Hills Pro Series Contour Kit Light in Light to Medium

☐ **Highlighter:** BECCA Shimmering Skin Perfector Pressed in Moonstone

BROWS

☐ **Colour:** Anastasia Beverly Hills Dipbrow Pomade in Taupe

EYES

☐ **Colour:** MAC Paint Pot in Painterly, and Urban Decay Gwen Stefani Eyeshadow Palette (Skimp, Anaheim and Punk)

☐ **Liner:** MAC Fluidline in Blacktrack

☐ **Mascara:** MAC Extended Play Lash mascara and Lord & Berry Back in Black mascara

☐ **False lashes:** Ardell Demi Wispies Black

LIPS

☐ **Liner:** MAC Cherry liner

☐ **Lipstick:** MAC lipstick in Dangerous

HAIR

☐ Baptiste hairspray

☐ Moroccanoil Glimmer Shine Spray

HAIR

~ Start with your hair. This look needs glamorous Hollywood waves so use a medium-size curling tong **(pic 1)** and then, starting at the back of the head, tong a 2–3 inch section and clip into a barrel curl to set whilst still warm **(pic 2)**.

~ Continue to do this, working up the head and round to the sides in horizontal sections. (Working vertically will produce a 1970s Farrah Fawcett-style wave, which you want to avoid!)

~ Leave the curls to cool for as long as you can – you can apply your make-up in the meantime – then gently comb through with a wide-tooth comb and apply hairspray into the waves. Use a spritz of Moroccanoil Glimmer Shine Spray for a glossy finish.

✄ **TOP TIP:** For a vintage twist, secure one side of the hair behind your ear with a clip and let the curls cascade over one shoulder.

BASE

~ Create a flawless base using a good moisturiser but avoiding the under-eye area. You can buy special hydrating creams to go under the eye which refresh the sensitive skin there and help to hydrate any fine lines, so concealer residue doesn't sit heavily within them. Apply this by patting a couple of dots onto each area and gently rub in.

~ Then prime the face using a good-quality matte primer, using your fingers to rub it in. Primer helps your make-up stay on for longer and reduces shine, so it is worth investing in (if you're after a more beachy-glow look, you can also get illuminating types that encourage a slight shimmer).

✄ **TOP TIP:** To eliminate redness use a green colour corrector. Colour correctors are great because instead of caking the skin in foundation you can essentially start with a blank skin canvas. Whether you're using green to combat redness, lavender to brighten sallow skin, or peach to neutralise dark circles under the eyes, there are paler and deeper intensities, so there's something

for every skin tone. For Lydia, who has a flushed complexion,
I use BECCA Backlight Targeted Colour Corrector in Pistachio.

FOUNDATION

~ This look is so contoured and flawless-looking, so a foundation
with great coverage is a must. Your foundation should be as close
to your natural skin tone as possible and, as it's sitting next to
your skin all day long, if there's one item you're going to splash
out on, make it this one. Create an airbrush effect by blending
in with a buffing brush.

CONCEALER

~ Create a light and clean contoured look under the eyes using
a concealer that's one or two shades paler than your skin colour.
Also apply down the middle of the nose and in the centre of
the forehead. I'd suggest blending in using a pointed foundation
brush.

POWDER

~ Set the foundation and concealer with a loose powder in a pale
pink or yellow colour.

CONTOUR

~ Use an angled brush to apply a mix of darker and warmer
shades (contour kits often include at least two of these) on and
below the cheekbones, around the hairline and lightly down
the sides of the nose. Build up the colour really gradually
and depending on how strong you want the effect to be.

BROWS

~ Use a colour that is as similar to your natural hair colour as
possible. If you want to really define your brows, then opt for a
shade that is slightly darker. I use Real Techniques 202 Angled

Liner to draw tiny fine hairs into the brows for natural definition. Enhance the brow you already have by filling out that shape, going right up to the end of the brow to give it a sharp edge.

EYES
~ Begin with a pale pink colour to knock out any darknesss **(pic 3)**. Then apply a pale satin shade, using a flat eyeshadow brush.
~ Contour the eye socket by first applying a matte light taupe-brown shade to the whole eyelid, then darken the outer socket edge using a darker shade **(pic 4)**.
~ Create the perfect eyeliner flick on the top lid by keeping the liner fine in the inner corner, following the curve of the lashline, and working out to a thicker flick. Lydia likes a high flick to lift and open her eyes **(pic 5)**.

LASHES
~ Apply a long-lasting mascara that doesn't clump – Lord & Berry Back in Black mascara is perfect for this.
~ Finish with false lashes to achieve a fuller, fluttery effect **(pic 6)**. If you have round eyes then you should look for ones where the lashes are more concentrated in the centre; if you have more of an almond eye shape, then look for one with a winged effect.

HIGHLIGHTER
~ Above the brow and cheekbone and under the eye apply an iridescent shimmery powder, then a pressed powder.

LIPS
~ For lasting coverage, pencil the entire lip in with lipliner before the lipstick **(pic 7)**. Lydia uses a cherry-coloured liner followed by a red lipstick **(pic 8)**.

✂ **TOP TIP:** If you mess up your liner, dip a flat brush like the C410 by Crown in concealer and tidy up the edges.

"

LOOK 2

BROWN SMOKY EYE, NUDE LIP AND BOUNCY BLOW-DRY

This one's superb for when I'm filming *TOWIE* or on an evening out with the girls. It's not too try-hard but looks really polished. As with look 1, below are the products I use in case you want to use them as a guide.

SHOPPING LIST

FACE

- ☐ **Moisturisers:** Origins Make A Difference Plus Rejuvenating Moisturiser; Emma Hardie Age Support Eye Cream
- ☐ **Primer:** Estée Lauder Matte Perfecting Primer and Rimmel Stay Matte Primer
- ☐ **Correctors and concealers:** BECCA Backlight Targeted Colour Corrector in Peach, and in Pistachio; Tarte Maracuja Creaseless Concealer in Medium Sand
- ☐ **Foundation:** Chanel Perfection Lumière Long-Wear Flawless Fluid in 30 Beige
- ☐ **Powder:** Bobbi Brown Sheer Finish Loose Powder in Pale Yellow
- ☐ **Baking:** Ben Nye Luxury Powder in Cameo
- ☐ **Blusher:** Urban Decay Gwen Stefani Blush Palette
- ☐ **Contouring:** Anastasia Beverly Hills Pro Series Contour Kit Light in Light to Medium

- ☐ **Highlighter:** MAC Mineralize Skinfinish in Soft & Gentle

BROWS

- ☐ **Colour:** MAC Fluidline Brow Gelcreme in Dirty Blonde

EYES

- ☐ **Colour:** MAC Cream Colour Base in Midtone Sepia; MAC Eye Shadow in Swiss Chocolate; MAC Eye Shadow in Embark; BECCA Shimmering Skin Perfector Pressed in Moonstone
- ☐ **Liners:** NARS Eye Paint in Black Valley; Urban Decay 24/7 Glide-On Eye Pencil in Roach
- ☐ **Mascara:** Benefit BADgal Lash mascara
- ☐ **False lashes:** Girls With Attitude Fantasy false lashes in Unicorn

LIPS

- ☐ **Liner:** Urban Decay 24/7 Glide-On Lip Liner in Liar
- ☐ **Lipstick:** MAC Cremesheen Glass in Boy Bait

HAIR

- ☐ Fudge 1 Shot Treatment Spray
- ☐ Fudge Big Hair Bodifying Style Whip
- ☐ Velcro rollers or pin curls

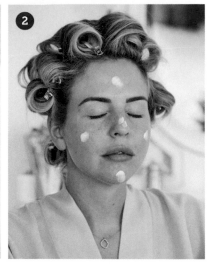

HAIR

~ Start with your hair so you can leave it to set whilst you do your make-up. For a smooth-finish bouncy blow-dry you need a hairdryer with a nozzle and a medium-sized round brush.

~ Wash your hair then blast off 70 per cent of the water. Apply a treatment spray to protect the hair, then a bodifying mousse to the roots. Remember that a little goes a long way: don't over-apply or it will make the hair feel tacky.

~ Start by parting your hair at the front, section off from the crown down to your ears, and clip the hair out the way. At the back of the head split the hair into two and take a 2-inch section. Wrap the hair around the brush and run the nozzle of the hairdryer back and forth down the hair shaft from roots to ends, whilst rolling the brush
up and down at the same time.

~ Once dry, pop a Velcro roller or pin curls into the section **(pic 1)**. Carry on all the way to the crown. Lydia likes her blow-dry to sit away from the front of her face; to do this take vertical sections and direct the hair back, away from the face.

~ Once the hair has cooled, remove the rollers and brush through with a soft brush, then back-comb at the crown using a small-tooth comb for greater volume.

BASE

~ Apply a light moisturiser to the face **(pic 2)**, using an eye cream under the eyes to achieve refreshed, puff-free skin.

~ Then opt for a primer that reduces shine and achieves a smooth, even finish.

FOUNDATION AND CORRECTOR

~ Using your ring finger (as this applies the lightest pressure) tap a peach tone under the eyes to eliminate dark circles, then tone down any redness and blemishes with a pistachio shade.

~ Use a sponge to apply a foundation that gives light and long-lasting coverage, which is very important for this look.

✂ **TOP TIP:** Before foundation, spray the sponge with a setting spray to give your make-up serious staying power

CONCEALER

~ Use your ring finger to dab concealer under the eyes and blend with a Beauty Blender sponge to achieve even coverage **(pic 3)**. This might feel like a lot of product but you need a light, bright and fresh undereye when creating a heavy, smoky look.

BAKING

~ This refers to the technique of letting translucent powder sit on your face for five to 10 minutes to allow heat from your skin to set your base foundation and concealer, then dusting the powder off for a creaseless, flawless finish. Dampen a small triangular sponge with fixing spray. Firmly place into a pale yellow loose powder, then press firmly under the eye before gently moving the sponge away, leaving a large amount of powder under the eye.

~ Repeat this three times to cover the entire undereye and leave to 'bake' while you apply your eye make-up **(pic 4)**.

BROWS

~ Define with a brow gel that matches or is darker than your eyebrow colour, using a small angled brush. Draw tiny, fine hairs into the brows for extra definition.

~ Brush out the beginning of the brow to give an ombre effect. This gives a subtle, multi-dimensional effect to boost thin brows.

EYES

~ Start with a creamy brown shade, sweeping over the entire lid **(pic 5)**. Then blend the socket line with a lighter, warmer colour **(pic 6)**. To pack on the colour and buff out the eye, darken the outer edge of the socket using a reddish-brown shadow.

~ Whitening the tear duct brightens and opens the eyes, so apply a pale shadow using a pencil brush, then a light yellow-tone highlighter.

~ If your choice of shadow is very dark you won't see eyeliner, so don't bother with it. But if you fancy a flick on the top lid, go for a small one using a black eyeliner pen or paint.

~ Line the undereye with a dark pencil **(pic 7)** then smudge it out with a pencil brush.

LASHES

~ Brush through with a voluminous mascara.

~ Then apply a strong false lash. One of Lydia's favourites is Girls With Attitude Fantasy in Unicorn.

CONTOUR

~ After dusting off the baking powder apply a mix of soft bronze matte and soft pink on and below the cheekbone, around the hairline and lightly down the sides of the nose **(pic 8)**. Build up the colour depending on how dark you want the shadow to be. Use a soft bronze on the cheekbone and soft pink just above it.

HIGHLIGHTER

~ Apply a medium highlight above the brow and cheekbone and under the eye with a light feathery brush to avoid over-application **(pic 9)**.

~ For extra-illuminated reflection, lightly dust a loose powder over the highlighter and cheeks. Opt for a shimmery, pearlescent powder for this.

LIPS

~ For staying power pencil in the entire lip with a nude shade.

~ Then top with a touch of pinky-beige gloss in the centre of the lips.

"

LOOK 3

GLOWY FRESH SKIN
AND BEACH WAVES

My go-to look for during the day when I'm popping to the shops, or if I've got meetings or day scenes on *TOWIE*. Here's my shopping list if you want a guide to products.

SHOPPING LIST

FACE

- [ ] **Primers:** Estée Lauder Illuminating Perfecting Primer and L'Oréal Lumi Magique Primer
- [ ] **Foundation:** NARS Stromboli Sheer Glow Foundation
- [ ] **Concealer:** NARS Custard Radiant Creamy Concealer
- [ ] **Powder:** Laura Mercier Secret Brightening Powder
- [ ] **Bronzer/Highlighers:** MAC Mineralize Skinfinish in Gold Deposit and Soft and Gentle

BROWS

- [ ] **Pencil:** Urban Decay Brow Beater Microfine Brow Pencil in Neutral Brown
- [ ] **Colour:** Benefit Gimme Brow Gel in Light/Medium

EYES

- [ ] **Eyeshadow:** NARS Irrésistiblement Bronzing Powder
- [ ] **Highlighter:** BECCA Shimmering Skin Perfector Pressed in Moonstone
- [ ] **Mascara:** Charlotte Tilbury Legendary Lashes mascara

LIPS

- [ ] **Liner:** Charlotte Tilbury's Lip Cheat Iconic Nude liner
- [ ] **Lipstick:** Urban Decay's Naked Ultra Nourishing Lip Gloss in Walk of Shame

HAIR

- [ ] Cloud Nine The Original Wand
- [ ] Tangle Teezer
- [ ] Batiste's Texture Me Texturising Spray.

BASE
~ Apply your moisturiser and then move onto primer. This look is all about glowing dewy skin so use an illuminating primer, like Estee Lauder Illuminating Perfecting Primer, which contains tiny light-reflecting particles for instant radiance

FOUNDATION
~ Make this glow go further by applying a hydrating, natural finish foundation (**pic 1**).

CONCEALER
~ Remember, this finish is super natural so concealer isn't a must but if you do want to cover a blemish opt for a creamy, lightweight concealer and build coverage (**pic 2**).

POWDER
Again remember – natural! Don't overdo the powder. Instead, dust the T-Zone (**pic 3**) with a transparent white powder.

CONTOUR
~ To maintain the beachy vibe lightly dust the highest points of the face – the hairline, forehead and cheekbones – with a soft reflective golden bronze (**pics 4 and 5**) using a fan brush to apply to the hairline and a rounder brush on the cheeks.

BROWS
~ Keep it soft and natural using a neutral colour (**pic 6**), then brush the hairs through with a brow comb and set with a light / medium brow gel.

EYES
~ For a soft, peachy tone, buff on a light bronzing powder with a blending brush then take it under the eye with a smaller pencil brush.

~ Use the same brush to dust a shimmering highlighter into the corner of the eye.

✄ **TOP TIP:** For a pencil brush that won't break the bank, try Morphe M431 precision brush.

~ There are no false lashes but lashings of mascara! To achieve a great natural lash Lydia loves Charlotte Tilbury Legendary Lashes mascara **(pics 7 and 8)**.

HIGHLIGHTER

~ For a soft and light finish dust the cheekbones using a pearlescent shade with a fan brush.

LIPS

~ Sheer, sheer, sheer! Line with a nude shade then use your finger to dab on a pale nude pink lip gloss **(pic 9)**.

HAIR

~ Beach waves are easy to achieve. Part freshly washed and dried hair into two sections then divide into smaller sections.

~ Starting from the nape of the neck use a large straightening iron like Cloud Nine The Original Wand and clamp the hair into the iron. As you run the iron through each piece of hair rotate it slowly. The slower you go, the looser the curl.

~ When you have a full head of curls, brush through with a Tangle Teezer then take random pieces and, using your thumb and forefinger, push the hair up from the middle to break up the curl and add texture.

~ Finish with a texture spray.

✄ **TOP TIP:** If your hair has a natural wave, use the wand to create extra wave to pieces that are slightly straighter.

,,

My style evolution!

50 shades of red
(okay, maybe just 5…)

One make-up trend I've rocked for years is a red lip and there's one woman to thank for that – my mum.

'Oh, that outfit would look sooo much better with red lips,' Mum would observe from the doorway of my bedroom whenever I was getting ready for a night out as a teenager. And here's a little secret – Debbie Douglas even sleeps in red lipstick, and only ever takes it off to clean her teeth!

Finding the perfect red lipstick isn't easy. It's like shopping for a pair of jeans – you've got to try a shedload of options before discovering the perfect fit. Type the words 'finding the right' into Google and it'll predict what you're looking for by what's popularly searched. After 'dog' and 'career' you'll see 'red lipstick'. See! The world is on the same hunt for the perfect rouge as you are.

1 **Rimmel Lasting Finish by Kate Moss, Shade 107 –** similar in shade to MAC Russian Red but creamy, so it doesn't dry out your lips. Also miles cheaper.

2 **MAC Ruby Woo –** the matte orange tones are perfect for a tanned summer complexion.

3 **Dior Diorific in Dolce Vita –** my brother Freddie bought this for me one Christmas, and I wear it whenever I'm around him. The creamy texture means it's best worn for just a couple of hours on a night out. And never when wearing white!

4 **MAC Russian Red –** a deep, matte, plummy tone and ideal when creating a sexy vintage evening look.

5 **Maybelline Super Stay 24hr Lip Colour in Ultimate Red –** this is my mum's everyday, must-have product. Iconic, stunning and does what it says on the tin by staining your lips for all-day kissable coverage.

✿ Make up break out ✿

These days I'm very particular about how I do my make-up. I've got very dry skin, and before my big *TOWIE* break in December 2010 I was so nervous and stressed over James that I developed terrible psoriasis, a skin condition that causes itchy red patches and is normally triggered by anxiety or a weak immune system. I'm therefore always mindful about the products I use on my face and body. The more natural and organic the better.

✿ On a role ✿

Having a positive influence on youngsters, particularly young girls, is important for me, because I know I'm a role model – and that's not me being bigheaded. Around 75 per cent of *TOWIE* viewers are female, and young girls can be influenced by what and who they see on the television. I know this because after *TOWIE* started national sales of fake tan and eyelashes went up! But while I think encouraging girls and young people to take pride in their appearance and look good – however shallow that sounds – can be a positive thing, I also think it's crucial that anyone in the public eye acts as a shining example to youngsters in other key areas. And that includes what's happening on the inside – starting with self-confidence . . .

#6
CONFIDENCE IS KEY

'YOU CAN DO IT, LYDS. MOVE YOURSELF, JUST LET LOOSE' INSTRUCTED SAM FAIERS FROM BEHIND THE PHOTOGRAPHER'S COMPUTER MONITOR, AS THE NEVER-ENDING STREAM OF IDENTICAL (AND AWKWARD) IMAGES FLASHED UP ON THE SCREEN.

Sam and I, along with a few of the other *TOWIE* girls – including Sam's sister Billie, Lucy Mecklenburgh, Jessica Wright and Lauren Goodger – were in a photographic studio called Holborn Studios in north London, on our first ever magazine photoshoot for *Now*. The theme was 'Christmas party' and all the girls were shining except – I was sure of it – me.

'Gorgeous! Beautiful!' enthused Nicky Johnston – a bald and bespectacled photographer who's worked with everyone from Justin Bieber to Joanna Lumley – with every explosion of the camera bulb. But rather than encouraging me, his compliments just made my heart sink a little bit deeper.

That day I felt like a fraud. Unlike Sam, who'd done a little bit of catalogue modelling in the past and was nailing every picture, I felt rigid and uncomfortable in front of the lens.

It's important to emphasise here that at this time there were physical differences between myself and the other *TOWIE* girls. They were all curvy, while I had what magazines would call a 'boyish' figure – straight up and down and athletic-looking – because I didn't grow boobs or develop a womanly bum, waist or hips until I was 23. Mum called me a 'late bloomer'. But my self-consciousness was nothing to do with the physical and everything about how I felt inside.

By then I was fully embracing vintage style. While my *TOWIE* pals loved bandeau dresses and sky-high heels, I felt uncomfortable in those sorts of clothes. Instead of being politely honest about how I wanted to look I'd say nothing as the hair and make-up artists and stylists followed the predictable *TOWIE* girl look: lashings of lashes, mascara and bronzer, plus tight, brightly coloured figure-hugging dresses.

Lauren Goodger was different. She never had a problem airing her feelings, and on the *Now* shoot, after her make-up was finished she said: 'I don't like what you've done. Can we change it?' I admired her honesty and ability to stand up for herself but I didn't feel able to. I'd been like that my whole life.

As a child, I changed primary schools twice, because I was painfully shy and struggled to fit in. In all my school reports teachers praised me for my academic ability but commented that I didn't contribute much in class and said I needed to stand up for myself more.

When I was a pupil at Snaresbrook Primary in Wanstead – I must have been about seven years old – a girl called Merella and I were playing hairdressers and using fake plastic scissors to 'chop off' our locks. Suddenly Merella darted across to the art department and fetched a pair of real shiny silver scissors, then began hacking off chunks of my lovely blonde hair.

At this point you should be reading that I screamed at Merella for being so stupid, but instead of stopping her I sat there and let her get on with it, tears filling my eyes as my golden hair fell to the floor of the classroom. I knew it was wrong of her but I was too shy to intervene.

'What on earth's happened to your hair!' shrieked Mum later that afternoon at the school gate on seeing the mess my barnet was in.

'Merella cut it,' I replied, bowing my head in shame as Mum inspected the jagged hack job.

'Why did you let her do that?!' she asked, incredulous.

'I didn't want to hurt her feelings,' I replied. And this was the problem.

Throughout my childhood, my fear of being assertive boiled down to not wanting to wound or annoy other people. Of course, it didn't matter that I was hurting myself in the process, which seems so silly now. Although I began to lose the disease to please in my early teens, it's only in the last six years, since establishing myself in *TOWIE* and running my own business, that I've discovered a new strength to speak my mind.

In the 2013 movie *The Love Punch* Emma Thompson's character says 'Just be yourself, honey' as her daughter leaves home to start a new life at college. But being ourselves is not always easy. Some people fear saying 'no' or 'I disagree' in case they're viewed as obstructive, but only when we do this will we earn respect in relationships, friendships, business and in every walk of life. It's called being true to ourselves!

❀ Imposter syndrome attacks ❀

If you're not brimming with self-confidence, don't panic, because you're not alone. In September 2012, during London Fashion Week, I was invited to take part in a panel discussion alongside fashion journalist Hilary Alexander and designer Olivia Rubin, who was just 25 when she set up her own fashion label, Olivia Rubin London.

The event took place at Somerset House in central London and the room was packed with fashion bloggers and press, who spent an hour listening to us chew the fat on topics including the social media influence on fashion, celebrities in fashion and starting a fashion business.

In the days leading up to the discussion and for the first few minutes on stage I was in a state of panic, asking myself questions like: 'What can I contribute? Why am I sat here next to such inspiring, intelligent and successful women? When will somebody realise I'm not as intelligent as they are?'

My guide to being true to yourself

Forget the lies. Don't like something? Then don't say you do! Don't want to go somewhere? Then don't commit, only to cancel later. Instead, be honest about your reservations from the start. You're in charge of your own feelings and life. People will respect that.

Don't act happy when you're secretly miserable. 'How are you?' is a question we're asked daily. But how many of us answer honestly? Why not be honest and say 'I'm not feeling that great today because . . .'? The chances are you'll get support you never anticipated.

Decide for yourself. These days advice arrives from all directions: Twitter, Facebook, family members, magazines. By all means, listen to other people's suggestions about how to live your life, but make your mind up for yourself. Your decisions are the ones you have to live with. Dig deep and decide how you truly feel.

Do away with dithering. Procrastination is avoidance, which is the surest sign that you secretly fear something. You can't be true to yourself if you circumnavigate your fears, so tap into what's worrying you and face it head on.

Tune in to your gut. You know those pit-of-the-stomach feelings that you can't ignore? That's called intuition, and is the best indication of how you truly feel. Apple founder Steve Jobs used to look in the mirror every morning and say: 'If today were the last day of my life, would I want to do what I'm about to do today?' If he answered 'no' too many days in a row he'd make a change to his life. The next time you have to make a decision, focus less on the facts and instead tap into your inner feelings. Chances are they will show you the right path!

Welcome to imposter syndrome – feelings of self-doubt that make you feel like a fraud. But here's the most intriguing thing: it's a condition that affects many of the world's most high-powered and high-flying women.

Facebook's chief operating officer Sheryl Sandberg once said: 'There are still days when I wake up feeling like a fraud, not sure I should be where I am.' Actress and UN Goodwill Ambassador Emma Watson has also admitted she feels like an imposter, and was secretly very nervous when she delivered a confident and intelligent inaugural speech on feminism at the UN summit in September 2014.

Other amazing females including Tina Fey, Kate Winslet, Renée Zellweger and Maya Angelou have said similar things, so the next time you feel a wobble of nerves – maybe it's your first day in a new job, or you're going on a first date or attending a party on your own – take reassurance from the fact that some of the world's most empowered women have grappled with feelings of self-doubt too. The truth is, a little self-doubt is not only normal, it's healthy, because it keeps you grounded. Just endeavour to deal with it in a constructive way!

All men love boobs. Really?

If there's one thing we're all guilty of from time to time it's letting our bodies get in the way of our self-confidence.

Apparently model and television presenter Kelly Brook had 32DD boobs by the age of 13. Some girls have all the luck, right?

I was deeply self-conscious about my body during puberty, when I was 12 or 13 and all my friends were developing boobs. Every week as we changed into our PE kit in the school changing rooms another girl would proudly show off the M&S bra she'd been fitted with over the weekend. I, meanwhile, remained flat as a pancake, no matter how many 'I must, I must, I must increase my bust' exercises (where I'd pull back my elbows to touch my back) I clocked up in my bedroom.

Growing up in Essex, I couldn't escape curves. Big boobs were all the rage, Page 3 seemed to be every schoolboy's obsession, and lads' mags like *FHM* and *Loaded* screamed one message: 'All men love boobs!'

By the time I was approaching my 16th birthday I'd had enough of my pigeon chest, so I sat my parents down in the kitchen, took a deep breath and made an announcement.

'Mum and Dad, I want a boob job for my 16th birthday present,' I said. The room was momentarily silent as Mum and Dad locked worried eyes.

'Lydia, darling . . .' Mum began, as Dad grunted and walked out the room, clearly uncomfortable with the conversation. On reflection, it can't have been easy for either of them hearing that I wanted cosmetic surgery at such a young age. I'm a product of them, their flesh and blood. I was basically saying: 'I'm not happy with your product – I want a refund!'

66 DRESSING FOR THE OPPOSITE SEX IS NO LONGER A TOP PRIORITY FOR ME 99

'Big boobs aren't fashionable,' said Mum, reaching over the table and holding my hands in hers. 'Wait until you're older before you make such a big decision about your body. You're still growing, and, trust me, you're beautiful just the way you are.'

I didn't believe her, but of course Mum was right. By the time I'd reached 18 I was content with my flatter chest and had stopped the boob job fantasies. None of the top fashion models I admired were big-chested, and some girls at school who'd had boob jobs at 17 were already regretting it.

In show business there's a lot of pressure to nip, tuck and enhance. Celebrity agents are often approached by cosmetic surgery companies offering free treatments for their clients in exchange for publicity. The conversation usually goes something like this:

'Hi, John. I've noticed that your client [insert name] isn't blessed in the boob department. How does [insert name] fancy a free boob job in exchange for talking about her surgery in interviews?'

My manager Kirsty has had many calls like this. One surgeon, who has treated reality stars including Amy Childs and *Geordie Shore*'s Charlotte Crosby and Holly Hagan, recently invited me to take my pick of the following: fillers, botox, a nose job, chin and cheek fillers and an eyebrow lift. I know . . . charming!

I'm proud to say that the only part of my body I've ever permanently changed are my teeth, by wearing braces when I was 13 and making them slightly whiter a few years back using peroxide gel. Other celebrities, however, have been sucked into a vicious cycle of cosmetic surgery and are constantly trying to perfect themselves, often tampering with body parts that didn't need changing in the first place.

Unfortunately, girls can often be too focused on appealing to the opposite sex and wrongly believe that guys won't look twice at them unless they've got perfect hips, boobs, bum and face.

Of course, I've tried to make myself attractive to men in the past – usually in the aftermath of a split, when I've craved a bit of male attention – but dressing for the opposite sex is no longer a top priority for me. I don't wear super-revealing or sexy clothes, and I don't dress for men. I actually get more of a buzz when a girl compliments me about my outfit.

Compliments are a cost-free and instant way to spread the love, so I dish them out as often as possible. If I'm in the ladies' loos and think a girl's outfit rocks, I tell her. If I'm in Tesco and see a woman with on fleek hair, I'll let her know. Compliments are powerful. They boost self-esteem and break down barriers. But in a Twitter-obsessed society criticism often rules, and I think it's sad that many of us have forgotten the art of high-fiving the sisterhood.

So here's a challenge – every day next week pay one stranger a genuine compliment. Trust me, it won't just make them feel good and brighten their day, it'll make you feel fabulous too!

✿ Invisible armour ✿

Although I've battled with shyness in the past, I've never felt insecure about who I am deep inside. Some of my friends won't leave the house before a night out until they've sent two mates a photo of their outfit for approval. I've never done that. I wear what I want to wear, I don't seek approval, and I've never asked a boyfriend 'Does this look nice?'

This sense of individuality was inspired from an early age by my mum, because she's not one to choose a well-trodden path. For example, she and my dad have been together for 37 years but are still unmarried, largely because they don't feel obliged to conform to what society expects.

Make no mistake. Being independently spirited takes courage. At school I was in the popular group where the 'cool' kids laid on peer pressure, encouraging me to be naughty, but (aside from that one time when I got drunk during lunch break) I refused to listen. I wanted to be clever and I wanted to study, so I'd spend my lunch breaks reading books in the library, which prompted some girls to walk past the window and shout: 'Loser!' Frankly, I didn't care because I was following my path, my dream. And look where it's got me! Criticism is something we all face in life and in recent years I've learned how to handle it. I've had to.

When I joined *TOWIE* I got so much stick from viewers, who despised me for tarnishing Arg's fun-loving reputation by saying he'd cheated on me. Although Lime Pictures had warned me about criticism, and I had sessions with a psychologist to gauge whether I'd be strong enough to cope with it, nothing could have prepared me for the level of abuse I received. Tweets slated my image and my physicality. I was called a 'dog', a 'drag queen' and 'ugly'. Some mocked my voice, declaring that I needed to blow my nose. Little did they know about the nasal issues I'd endured as a child.

Being an Aquarius, I always endeavour to see the best in everyone, but those Twitter trolls were devilish and hurt me with what they wrote. In the early days I'd respond, firing back angry messages in a desperate bid to be understood. Of course, this was a mistake. Social media bullies are just looking for a reaction, so silence is the best form of defence.

❀ Little Miss Fit ❀

Not long after that first photoshoot for *Now* magazine the press began comparing my 'straight up, straight down' size 6–8 body to the more curvaceous physiques of my *TOWIE* co-stars. Some articles even declared that I was too skinny, and in hindsight they were probably right.

I've always had an athletic frame, the result of ballet dancing from the age of three, and modern, street and cheerleading dancing until I was in my teens. But during my first year on *TOWIE*, I was getting used to fame, constantly on the go and dealing with all the stress of dating James in the public eye.

The life mantras that make me...me!

'Some people are settling down, some people are settling and some people refuse to settle for anything less than butterflies' *Carrie Bradshaw*

This nugget from my *Sex and the City* life idol serves as a reminder that love is so beautiful and exciting, but if a relationship isn't fulfilling your heart and soul, never be afraid to walk away.

'Imperfection is beauty, madness is genius and it's better to be absolutely ridiculous than absolutely boring' *Marilyn Monroe*

I couldn't agree more with this saying from Marilyn, actress, model and life-inspirer! My mum has always been eccentric, broken the mould and paved her own path in life by doing things her way. I'd hate nothing more than to lead a boring existence, so I pledge from here on in to follow suit, living life my way!

'Travel while you're young and able. Don't worry about the money, just make it work. Experience is far more valuable than money will ever be' *Unknown*

I found this quote on Instagram and I wish I knew who wrote it so I could shake their hand. I've always been an explorer. It's so easy to turn down trips and put dream destinations on hold because of work commitments or financial struggles. But don't miss your opportunity to see the world while you can. Sacrifice that morning coffee or dinners out and save the money, but, most importantly, find the time to create memories that will last a lifetime.

'Nothing is impossible, the word itself says "I'm possible"!' *Audrey Hepburn*

I LOVE LOVE LOVE fashion and film icon Audrey – her style, her class and her humanitarian work. This quote sums up my approach to life and love: nothing is out of reach. So set your goals and follow your heart. Then reach for the stars!

'In life we do things. Some we wish we had never done. Some we wish we could replay a million times in our heads. But they all make us who we are, and in the end they shape every detail about us' *Anonymous*

This quote is so insightful and urges us to never regret what's happened in the past because we all have ups and downs. Every step we take is part of our journey, our story and the making of us. The key message I take from this is to always live for the moment . . . and the future!

'It's very important to take risks. I think that research is very important, but in the end you have to work from your instinct and feeling and take those risks and be fearless' *Anna Wintour*

Remember my advice about following your gut instinct? Well, thank you Anna Wintour for hammering home the point! Anna is one of the most important and influential women in the fashion world, reportedly worth £25 million, and since she became the editor-in-chief of American *Vogue* in 1988 she switched the culture of fashion into something all young women were inspired by. I truly admire her.

'The world is full of wonderful things you haven't seen yet. Don't ever give up on the chance of seeing them' *J. K. Rowling*

Novelist and screenwriter J. K. has one of the most imaginative minds on the planet and millions of children travelled to a different world by reading Harry Potter (although sorry J.K., I wasn't one of them!). The real world is vast and beautiful and travelling teaches us independence, appreciation of other cultures and how to live in the present. Close your eyes and pick a place on the map to visit – go on, I dare you!

'Do not let the behaviour of others destroy your inner peace' *the Dalai Lama*

Too often what other people do and say makes us feel angry and hurt. But the truth is nobody can *make* us feel anything. We're the only ones in charge of our own mental states. The next time you feel angry or hurt, talk yourself down into a calmer place. Brush it off and carry on with your happiness.

During this time, there was another reason for my slim physique – lack of food. Missing meals was never something I did on purpose. I never had an eating disorder but I'd regularly forget to eat meals, and often 6 p.m. would roll around after a hard day's filming and I'd think: 'Oh my God, I've not eaten today.'

Looking back, surviving on so few calories was irresponsible. But the problem wasn't a deliberate desire to deprive myself of food, merely a lack of structure to my life. Before *TOWIE* I had a schedule so I'd eat at set meal times, be it at school, in an office or at the bar in Marbella. Suddenly, I was so busy with meetings, work and general life that my good intentions to eat accidentally disappeared and I dropped over a stone very quickly.

Over the years my female co-stars (girls like Lucy Meck, Frankie Essex and Lauren Goodger) have slimmed down after acquiring personal trainers and adopting a healthier attitude to nutrition. Meanwhile, my dress size has gone up, and this is also thanks to a healthy lifestyle where nutritional food and fitness have become a daily focus.

I hated PE at school. The prospect of getting sweaty then putting my uniform back on and spending a day feeling unclean filled me with dread. But I was always an active child. I loved dancing and Mum didn't believe in ferrying us around by car so we always walked everywhere. During my A levels I dropped dancing – I couldn't commit to the weekly classes with set assignments and coursework mounting – but shortly after leaving school I got my first gym membership.

I've never been a hardcore gym bunny but I now go three or four times a week and I love both the physical and emotional rewards. Working out triggers feel-good endorphins, puts a smile on my face and injects me with energy that lasts all day. On the flip side, when I miss gym sessions I feel fatigued and less likely to stick to a healthy diet, so I get frustrated and moody. Even after a big night and only three hours sleep I feel like I can conquer the world following a workout. Getting into an exercise routine can take months, but once you click into it and develop a love/love relationship with exercise you'll never look back. Unfortunately, there's no magic spell to get you there. It's simply perseverance, willpower and effort!

On average, it takes more than two months before a new behaviour becomes a habit — 66 days to be exact. So, stick to a gym plan for two months and *voilà*! You'll be into your exercise groove.

Go figure

The NHS recommends at least 150 minutes of moderate aerobic activity, such as cycling or fast walking, every week, plus twice-weekly strength exercises to work major muscles in the legs, hips, back, abdomen, chest, shoulders and arms. It sounds like a lot but it's doable. Obviously, we'd all love to have enough time every day to devote to a workout, a relaxing swim, steam room and Jacuzzi, but our commitments to work, school, college and our social lives often mean our time is squeezed.

My advice is that every little helps, so avoid thoughts like 'There's no point' when you're pushed for time or lacking motivation. A 20-minute run on the treadmill is better than nothing!

A fun event on the horizon can be a great fitness target, such as a wedding, a birthday party, a work function or a summer holiday. Ahead of my return to *TOWIE* in April 2014, which was set to be filmed in Marbella, I set myself the ultimate challenge – to transform my body.

I hired a personal trainer and for five weeks dedicated myself to daily exercise and followed a strict healthy-eating plan (including no alcohol). It was tough – and unsustainable – but knowing it was for the short term kept me motivated!

By the time I was in Marbella ready to make my comeback my body was the best it's ever been. I had the flattest stomach of my life (complete with abs), my upper legs, back, shoulders and arms were ripped, and I'd dropped a dress size.

My friend Dr Zoe Williams, an exercise expert who used to be on Sky 1's *Gladiators* (she was Amazon, to save you googling), has recreated my exercise routine for you guys to do at home. It's a total HIIT (high-intensity interval training) workout, which uses a combination of cardio and resistance to burn fat and tone the muscles. You do each exercise for one minute and push yourself to the max during that time, then enjoy a one-minute rest in between each move.

The best thing about HIIT is you continue to burn calories for 24 hours after the workout, and you don't need a gym so you can do it anywhere – the park, your garden, your living room or even in your hotel room if you're away on holiday or business.

I can't promise you'll achieve the exact results I did in 2014 because every body is different, but I know that if you combine the moves with a healthy eating plan you'll look and feel brilliant in a month. Good luck!

Fitness focus – my top tips for workout motivation

1 **Eat bananas.** They're full of an amino acid called tryptophan, which converts into a mood stabilising chemical, serotonin. Eating a banana before a strenuous workout will get you in the zone. It'll also boost your energy levels by sustaining blood sugar.

2 **Invest in a gorgeous gym kit.** We all feel more inspired to leave the house when we look good, and heading to the gym is no exception. Rosie Huntington-Whiteley's fitness range at M&S is beautiful, and you can't go wrong with New Look for great-value kit. And always invest in a good pair of trainers to protect your joints and ligaments. I wear Nike Free Run trainers in the gym because they're breathable, lightweight and look good!

3 **Don't burn out.** Contestants on shows like *The Biggest Loser* spend hours a day exercising, which is fine when you're on the show, but doesn't really translate into real life. You'll resent the time you spend on exercise and soon lose the buzz. Little and often is better than overdoing it.

4 **Use Insta-piration.** Don't get fixated with other people's body shapes but do start following a few fitness experts on Instagram to encourage you. I find mum and gym-obsessed @sarahstage inspiring, and I also follow Squats On Squats (@squatspo) which shows lots of amazing bums and exercise videos. I like working on my bum because it's my most womanly part.

5 **Reward yourself.** That smoothie, those shoes, tickets to your favourite festival. When you've worked hard in the gym you should treat yourself. Go on, you're worth it.

BEFORE YOU START ...

✶ If you have any injuries or concerns about exercising, always consult your doctor first.

✶ Make sure you warm up for at least 10 minutes. This doesn't have to be anything strenuous: you can alternate marching on the spot with jogging on the spot, lunges and squats. The idea is to get your muscles feeling warm and loose.

AND AFTER YOU FINISH . . .

✶ Stretching AFTER exercise is important to prevent injuries and maximise range of motion.
✶ Aim to stretch the main large muscle groups – quads, hamstrings, calves, neck, chest, shoulders and lower back. Each stretch should be held for 20–30 seconds.
✶ Don't forget to use this as time to reflect on the great work that you have just done and allow your breathing to slow down and become relaxed again.

V

LYDIA'S 24-MINUTE BODY BLAST

Remember – do each exercise as hard as you can for one minute, then rest for one minute.

1 JUMPING JACKS

THE MOVE: Start with your feet together and arms by your sides, then jump feet apart while your arms go up and out to make a star shape, then jump back to the original position, and repeat.

THE RESULTS: An all-over workout, great for warming up the body and getting the blood pumping.

2 BACKWARD LUNGE, ARMS ABOVE HEAD

THE MOVE: With arms up above your head, step your right foot out behind you and lunge down so that your right knee touches the ground, then come back to standing position. Repeat, alternating between right and left.

THE RESULTS: Strengthens and tones legs, buttocks and core. Improves hip flexibility.

3 BACK RAISE INTO PUSH-UP

THE MOVE: Start by lying on your tummy, and lift your hands and feet backwards up into the air, arching your back. Then return to a lying position, put your hands flat under your shoulders and do a full push-up. If you can't do a push-up balancing on your toes, balance on your knees. But do attempt the harder movement. You don't get better unless you try!

THE RESULTS: Strengthens lower back muscles. Great for getting rid of lower back pain. Push-up tones arms, chest and core.

4 STARFISH CRUNCH

THE MOVE: Lie on your back with arms and legs out in a star shape. Touch your left toe with your right hand, whilst keeping your left shoulder on the ground. Alternate with the other side.

THE RESULTS: Strengthens abdominal muscles, especially the obliques.

5 BURPEE TO TUCK JUMP

THE MOVE: Place your hands on the ground in front of your feet, jump your feet back into a press-up position, jump feet forwards again and then stand and go straight into a tuck jump.

THE RESULTS: Works the whole body.

6 TRICEP DIP HIP LIFT

THE MOVE: Have a sturdy chair, bench or step behind you that won't move, sit with your hands on it beside your hips, then push your hips forwards, legs straight in front, so that your arms are supporting your body weight. Bend your elbows so that your body dips back down, then push your arms straight to come back up, pushing your hips towards the ceiling/sky. Repeat.

THE RESULTS: Banishes bingo wings.

7 LIE TO JUMP STAND

THE MOVE: American football-style, stand with your feet hip-width apart, bend your knees and squat down slightly; then, keeping your feet wide, run on the spot as fast as you can, then drop to the ground, lie on your tummy, get up again and launch into a jump. Repeat.

THE RESULTS: Works the whole body.

8 FULL-V SIT-UP

THE MOVE: Lie on your back, arms up above your head; then, keeping feet together and hands together, lift them all up towards the sky and touch your toes, making a V-shape off the ground.

THE RESULTS: Strengthens abdominals and core.

> 66 THIS WORK-OUT IS LESS THAN 2% OF YOUR DAY – SO YOU CAN DO THIS! 99

9 SQUAT INTO ALTERNATE LATERAL LUNGES

THE MOVE: Starting with feet hip-width apart, push your hips back and bend at the knees to do a deep squat. As you come up, jump your right leg out to the side and lower into a deep sideways lunge, return back to feet hip-width apart and squat, then lunge sideways to the other side. Repeat.

THE RESULTS: Works the whole body, especially legs and buttocks.

10 MOUNTAIN CLIMBERS

THE MOVE: Start in press-up position, hands directly below your shoulders. Lift your right foot off the ground and raise your knee as close as possible to your chest, return to start position, then repeat, alternating sides.

THE RESULTS: Works the whole body.

11 HIP BRIDGE WITH KNEE SQUEEZE AT TOP

THE MOVE: Lie on your back, knees bent, feet flat on the floor. Raise your hips off the floor, so your body is in a straight line from shoulders to knees. Squeeze your knees together, then slowly go back to lying on your back. Repeat.

THE RESULTS: Strengthens the bottom, back and inner legs and core. This is an excellent exercise if you have back injuries.

12 FINISHER: SPLIT LUNGE JUMP ALTERNATE

THE MOVE: Start with feet hip-width apart, and one a foot-and-a-half in front of the other. Your front foot should be flat on the floor, your back foot on the ball/front part of the foot. Sink down, then explosively jump up, swapping your feet over in mid-air, and sink down again, then keep switching.

THE RESULTS: Works the whole body, especially the fronts of the legs and the buttocks.

Everyday toning moves (no excuses!)

But of course, you don't always need to do a whole exercise routine. These toning moves can be incorporated into your everyday life. So bad news, ladies. No excuses!

Telly toner: While watching your favourite TV show, perch against the wall as if you're sitting on an invisible chair. It burns like mad after 20 minutes and really works your glutes.

Thigh chopper: You spend two minutes every morning and night cleaning your teeth, so use the time to tone your thighs. While brushing your top teeth balance on one leg and squat up and down, then shift to the other leg while scrubbing your bottom ones.

Teatime tricep dips: While waiting for the kettle to boil, grip the kitchen work surface while facing out, keep your feet together and legs straight, lower your body straight down slowly and press back up. Keep your bottom as close to the counter as possible and your elbows pointing back and your back straight. Repeat until the kettle's boiled.

Bum blaster: Clench your bum tightly when you walk (obviously not while wearing leggings or a super-tight dress), as if you've got a walnut between your butt cheeks. It'll tone your butt without you even realising!

Core blimey: At work adjust your desk chair height so your feet, hips, and arms are at 90-degree angles to the floor. Engage your core and stay slouch-free all day.

🌸 Food, glorious food 🌸

Feeling and looking good starts on the inside. I never deny myself a bit of what I like to eat (pasta, pizza and pie and mash are my biggest downfalls, especially when hung-over), but because I work out on exercise machines that reveal how many calories I've burned I think carefully about what I eat. Put it this way – one slice of chocolate cake takes 20 minutes of hard slog on the treadmill, so I'd rather skip the cake and spend my time chilling on the sofa!

I took part in a four-part celebrity version of *The Island with Bear Grylls* in February 2016 to raise money for Stand Up to Cancer (you can find out all the gossip in the next chapter!), and the experience transformed my relationship with food. I was 9st 5lb when I started, the heaviest I'd been in a long time because I'd gorged on food ahead of the challenge, knowing it would be in short supply. For eight days I survived without eating a morsel, and by the end of the two weeks I was one and a half stone lighter.

❝ FEELING AND LOOKING GOOD STARTS ON THE INSIDE ❞

My taste buds have never been the same. Before *Celebrity Island* I rarely ate sweet foods or fruit and loved homely, carbohydrate-rich dinners like curries and my nan's macaroni cheese. During the challenge I craved flavoursome, sugar-rich fruits like bananas and berries and I now can't stomach massive carb-laden dinners because they leave me feeling sluggish. These days I eat little and often and feel all the better for it.

At my home in Essex my fridge and kitchen cupboards are stocked with delicious, nutritious ingredients to make healthy meals and snacks. Cooking from scratch stops us reaching for convenient ready-made meals, many of which are not only over-priced but are packed with excess sugar and salt.

RECIPES
FOR SUCCESS

Family feeding is an Italian thing and from as early as I can remember Sundays were family 'cook-out' days, when my aunts, uncles, cousins – even our neighbours – would flock to our house. Nanny Maureen spent hours slaving over the stove, preparing cauldrons of sausage casserole, minestrone soup, macaroni cheese and lasagne.

Nanny Maureen is a professional cook and is my favourite chef ever. Some of my fondest memories from childhood are of us baking together. We used to make Victoria sponge, lemon drizzle cake and buttercream cupcakes, but these days, because I'm not such a big cake fan, I'm most inspired by her delicious savoury recipes.

I cook from scratch probably about four times a week and love posting pictures of my creations on Instagram. Here are some of my favourite recipes for you to create at home . . .

My Budget Luxury Muesli

Muesli is my favourite breakfast. It's nutrient-rich, full of fibre, protein, healthy fats and carbohydrates. Oh, and it's delicious too! Luxury brands are pricey so I've created my own cost-saving homemade version. The best bit is that you're in charge of the ingredients, so you can mix and match whatever takes your fancy. Store in a big plastic airtight cereal container and serve daily, knowing you've saved yourself a few pennies by making your own.

* *

Makes approx 20 portions
Preparation time: 10 minutes

Ingredients:
1kg rolled oats
200g dried apricots
200g dried blueberries
200g raisins
200g walnuts (chopped)
70g sunflower seeds
75g sesame seeds

In a large bowl, mix the oats with the apricots, blueberries, raisins, walnuts and seeds, using your fingers to mix it. Store in an airtight container.

Serve with a drizzle of honey and drenched in milk or, for a sweeter alternative, soya milk.

TOP TIP
MAKE A MUESLI SMOOTHIE BY MIXING IN A BLENDER WITH CHUNKS OF FROZEN BANANA, FOR EXTRA CHILL AND SWEETNESS. DELISH!

Prawn and Veg Stir-Fry

Cooking for one isn't much fun (food is nicer when it's shared, right?) but this super-quick, healthy and wholesome recipe will inject a bit of variety into your weekly dinner plans if, like me, you reach all too often for that convenient tin of soup. I make this at least once a week and it's perfect for after a workout, a long day at work, or whenever you're starving and can't wait a moment to eat!

✳✳✳

Serves 1
Preparation and cooking time:
17 minutes

Ingredients:
1 tbsp olive oil
½ red pepper, chopped
  into chunks
½ onion, chopped into chunks
4 x sliced cup mushrooms
1 carrot, topped and tailed
  and peeled
Handful of bean sprouts
1 tbsp oyster sauce
2 tbsp soy sauce
1 tbsp chilli flakes (or fresh
  chilli if you have it)
Pinch of salt
100g peeled prawns
  (fresh or frozen)

Add olive oil to a wok and bring to medium heat. Chuck in the pepper, onion and mushrooms.

Use a potato peeler to make carrot ribbons. Add to the pan with the bean sprouts.

Add the oyster sauce, soy sauce, chilli flakes and salt, cook for one minute.

Throw in the prawns and toss until they turn pink (you can also use chicken if preferred). Eat immediately and mentally high-five yourself because it tastes amazing.

My Tasty Thai Green Curry

I picked up this recipe in Chiang Mai, Thailand's northern capital, when I was travelling with my sister. One day we took a cooking class, where we learned to make spring rolls, pad Thai and a number of curries. This was my favourite recipe of all. I love spice, and the flavours are out of this world. I like to cook this for a romantic date or dinner party because it's very impressive. You'll need a pestle and mortar to make the paste.

Serves 2 hungry people
Preparation and cooking time:
45 minutes

Ingredients:
300ml coconut milk
2 tbsp olive oil or vegetable oil
350g diced chicken breast
1 aubergine, chopped into
   1cm cubes
1 red pepper, finely chopped
2 red chillies, thinly sliced
   (add more if you like spice)
5 basil leaves, torn
2 tbsp fish sauce
1 tbsp palm sugar

For the curry paste:
1 tbsp coriander seeds
2 green chillies, finely chopped
   (add more if you like spice)
1 lemongrass stalk, finely
   chopped
3 kaffir lime leaves
Galangal (sugar cube amount)
Turmeric (sugar cube amount)
2 cloves garlic, peeled and
   finely chopped
1 shallot, finely chopped

First, bring a pan of water to the boil and begin cooking your rice (I use boil in the bag) according to the instructions on the packet.

Prepare your curry paste. Grind the coriander seeds into a powder using a large pestle and mortar.

Add the remaining spices one by one, followed by the garlic and then the shallot. Pound each one as it is added to create a smooth paste.

Next, pour the coconut milk into the wok and cook on a high heat until oil appears on the surface.

Add your curry paste and stir together. Leave to simmer for 15 minutes on a low heat.

Add oil to a frying pan and bring to a high heat. Fry off the chicken until brown then add the aubergine, red pepper, red chillies and basil leaves and fry until the chicken is cooked through.

Put the meat and veg into the wok containing your curry paste and coconut milk combo, then add fish sauce and palm sugar and simmer for a few minutes. Serve with the rice. *Voilà!* An easy and tasty supper, sorted!

Pie, Mash And Liquor

You don't get more of a traditional Essex/east London dish than pie and mash (it's David Beckham's favourite). FYI, liquor isn't alcoholic – it's a savoury parsley sauce. This dish is the ultimate stodgy feed and is my ultimate hangover cure. My favourite pie-and-mash shop is the famous Robins in Wanstead, which has been following the same recipe for five generations. This is a dish I cook up for a girlfriend for a hungover weekend lunchtime.

Serves 2
Preparation and cooking time: 1 hour

For the pie:
2 tbsp olive oil
400g lean minced beef
100ml beef gravy
100ml beef stock
2 tbsp flour
Salt
Pepper
Jus-Rol shortcrust pastry
　　block (320g)
1 egg, beaten

For the mash:
2 large potatoes, peeled
　　and cubed
40g butter

For the liquor:
50g butter
50g cornflour
600ml chicken stock
10 parsley leaves, finely chopped
Pinch of salt
1 tbsp malt vinegar

Preheat the oven to 200°C/gas mark 6.

Heat the oil in a frying pan and add the mince. Toss until brown. Add the beef gravy, beef stock and flour. Stir until the liquid is bubbling. Season with salt and pepper then pop on a pan lid and take off the heat. Leave to stand for 30 minutes so the meat absorbs all the yummy flavour.

Roll out the pastry, place the pie dishes top-downwards, and cut two pieces big enough to top each dish. Fill the pie dishes with the mince mixture. Place the pastry over the top then lightly brush with beaten egg and prick two holes in the pastry. Bake for 25 minutes in the oven.

For the mash, add chopped potatoes to a pan of salted water and boil for around 20 minutes, until the potatoes are soft. Drain, add the butter, then mash.

Meanwhile, for your parsley liquor melt the butter in a saucepan and add cornflour, then whisk to make a paste. Add chicken stock, parsley, salt and malt vinegar, and stir until thick and smooth.

Leave the pies to stand for 2 minutes before serving to allow the pastry to settle. Serve with the mash and liquor.

Nanny's Lasagne

❧ ❧ ❧ ❧ ❧

*Lasagne was a staple in our family home, where my nan did a lot of cooking
(Mum's not great in the kitchen!), and this is her signature dish. She often cooked
it for Grandad after his mother, Lina, taught her all her culinary tricks. Nan
taught me the recipe when I was 14 and now I cook it for the family.*

✳ ✳

Serves 6
**Preparation and
cooking time: 2 hours 45
minutes**

Ingredients:
2 tbsp olive oil
1kg lean minced beef
1 onion, finely chopped
2 cloves garlic, peeled and
    finely chopped
2 carrots, peeled and
    finely chopped
2 tbsp tomato purée
2 x 400g tins chopped tomatoes
4 basil leaves, torn
400g pasta sheets
Parmesan cheese

For the béchamel sauce:
300ml milk
30g butter
30g flour

Heat the oil in a large frying pan. Add and cook the mince, gently tossing until it goes brown. Turn the heat to low and add the onion, garlic, carrots, tomato purée, chopped tomatoes and basil. Remove from the heat, cover, and leave for 2 hours to infuse and marinate.

Soak the pasta sheets in hot water and leave on a clean rack for 1 hour.

Preheat the oven to 180°C/gas mark 4.

To make your béchamel sauce, add the milk to a saucepan and bring to the boil. Melt the butter in a frying pan and mix in the flour until it forms a paste. Add the paste to the milk and stir over a gentle heat for roughly 5 minutes until you get a smooth sauce.

In a baking dish add a layer of mince mixture, top with grated Parmesan cheese, then a layer of lasagne sheets, then a layer of béchamel sauce. Then add another layer of mince and follow the same formula twice more. After laying the final lasagne sheet add béchamel sauce and lots of Parmesan cheese. Put in the oven for 1 hour, or until the top is golden and the mince around the edge is bubbling.

Leave to stand for 20 minutes before serving (patience is a virtue here!). For an even better flavour, refrigerate overnight before baking – it's always tastier the next day!

Snack attack

Carry these healthy treats in your handbag to zap hunger and stop you reaching for the Haribo.

Rice cakes: Snack a Jacks do so many flavours, including salt-and-vinegar, caramel and chocolate, so whether you've got a sweet tooth or a savoury one there's an option for you. Never reach for crisps again!

Popcorn: I go through loads and it's virtually calorie-free. It's also cheap to make. Result!

Jelly: It's just 60p for a pack and I combine it with fruit, then leave it to chill in pretty vintage tea cups. It's a taste of childhood.

Boiled eggs: I carry them in their shell in a Tupperware tub. They're high in protein so are great to munch on before a workout.

Nuts: They're full of omega-3 fats so are brilliant for your heart and for lowering cholesterol. A 30g portion (golf-ball size) is all you need.

*Food is essential
to life, therefore
make it good*
(S. Truett Cathy)

🌹 Girl power with pout 🌹

All the girls in the first series of *TOWIE* inspired me. Sam, Billie, Lauren Goodger and Lucy were business-savvy, ruthless, brilliant and confident. In the same way my mum was inspired by Goggie Troughton when she was 18, when I joined *TOWIE* I fed off these powerful women – and they helped bring me out of my shell. Collectively, they taught me a valuable lesson: 'Those who are quiet will be forgotten.'

So as I got more established in my career, my confidence grew and so did my voice. In my personal and professional life I became increasingly able to be honest about my opinions, express myself when I felt something wasn't right, and big myself up when it mattered, like in interviews and business meetings. My confidence has been nourished by achievement, success and experience and if I could go back in time and give my 18-year-old self a pep talk I'd say: 'Don't compare yourself to others, embrace your uniqueness, practise saying 'no' in the mirror (you'll need that word a lot to stand up for what you truly believe in), listen to your intuition (it's the best advisor you have), and whatever disappointment, betrayal, heartbreak and hurt you experience, nothing is forever and everything is going to be okay.

When I think back to that first *TOWIE* photoshoot for *Now* I just smile, because I know I've come so far in mind, body and spirit. When I do group photoshoots now with the *TOWIE* girls I'm the one stood behind the photographer's monitor encouraging the newbies to be the best they can be, just like Sam Faiers did with me all those years ago. Now I have the chance to go one step further and share the passion, the knowledge and the lessons I've learned on my amazing journey with you guys too . . . and that makes me feel amazing.

#7
CLIMB EVERY MOUNTAIN

MY GRANDAD LOU'S 20-A-DAY
CIGARETTE HABIT STARTED WHEN HE
WAS JUST EIGHT YEARS OLD. I KNOW,
HOW SHOCKING IS THAT?

But growing up in a little Italian town called Loreto in the late 1940s, nobody cared or probably even knew about the risks of smoking tobacco. Puffing on fags was as normal as chewing a stick of gum. Even though Grandad smoked every day of his life, drank a bottle of red wine every night, had hardly any teeth and skin like leather, he was a slim and fit decorator who loved breakdancing to my favourite rap music! Even at the age of 60. We always joked that Nanny Maureen, who remains the epitome of good health, would ironically be the first to pop her clogs. To me Grandad Lou seemed invincible. How naive was I?

In June 2004, when I was 13 years old, Grandad began feeling unwell. Doctors diagnosed flu, but three weeks or so later, when he was still poorly, he was rushed to hospital for tests. The results hit our family with bulldozer force.

One afternoon after school Mum called me and Georgia into the kitchen and broke the news.

'Your grandad's very sick,' she said, and I could see her eyes filling with tears. 'He's not got long to live so it's important we spend as much time as possible with him while we still can.'

Grandad, who was 64, had lung cancer. The ciggies had finally got the better of him. Tests revealed that his whole body was riddled with the disease, and there was no hope. Grandad was going to die, and once he knew that his illness was terminal he lost his energy, his zest for life . . . his fighting spirit.

Grandad returned from hospital because he wanted to spend his last few days in the comfort of his own bed. At the time I was staying with my grandparents for the summer holidays, so to give Grandad space Nanny shared my bed, which was nice but sad too. Sometimes at night when she thought I was asleep I'd hear her crying for Grandad.

The end came on Monday 19 July 2004, four weeks after the diagnosis, and all I remember of that day is my mum, my Auntie Jackie and my Uncle Jason going into Grandad's bedroom to dress him in his favourite suit. He'd been a lifelong scruffy dresser and they refused to let him make his final journey in a white vest and ripped jeans.

Sometimes Mum mourned Grandad so hard that she couldn't get out of bed, and there was no way she was strong enough to do a reading at the funeral so Georgia and I volunteered to read a poem we'd written together. It was a beautiful service but understandably a very traumatic moment for our family. To this day I can't listen to Elvis's 'Always On My Mind' – my grandad's favourite song – without welling up. It played as his coffin was carried out of the church to be buried.

We were all so shocked by my grandad's decision to be buried in England, because for years he'd banged on about wanting to be buried in Loreto next to his mum and nan. In his dying days Grandad's wish changed, and he was laid to rest in Maldon in Essex, the seaside town where he and my nan lived, with space left beside him for Nanny to one day join him.

My grandparents fought terribly over the years, but deep down there was so much love and that really surfaced in his final days.

Knowing that I'd never see Grandad again hurt like hell. You never know when you'll say 'hello' or 'goodbye' to a loved one for the last time. How scary is that?

Losing Grandad to cancer was my primary motivation for taking part in *Celebrity Island with Bear Grylls*, in aid of the big fundraising campaign Stand Up to Cancer, which aired on

Channel 4 in October 2016. The whole campaign raised £15.7 million for Cancer Research UK.

I've raised money for lots of different causes over the years, including the mental health charity Mind, the breast cancer charity CoppaFeel!, the Vipingo Village Fund in Kenya, and Great Ormond Street Hospital. Doing something to benefit Cancer Research UK to help fight the disease that stole my grandad felt good, and I know he would have been so proud of me.

🌹 Teaming up with Bear 🌹

'You've been approached to take part in a charity version of *The Island with Bear Grylls*,' announced Kirsty when I answered the phone one chilly morning in November 2015 as the rain pelted down like bullets outside my bedroom window.

'Two weeks living on a tropical island?' I replied. 'Where do I sign?!'

Shine TV, the production company behind all the Bear Grylls television shows, had contacted Lime Pictures to ask if a *TOWIE* cast member would be up for spending two weeks battling the elements on a remote island in Panama, which is a country sandwiched between North and South America.

My name was suggested along with a few others, including Arg, James Lock and Jessica Wright, but I was the first to get in front of the show's talent executive, a lovely chap called David Allberry. Unfortunately, that scuppered it for everyone else on the shortlist.

'Lydia, you're perfect for this show,' enthused David during my interview, shutting his notebook where he'd made copious notes as I talked enthusiastically about charity challenges I'd done in the past.

'We're not going to interview any more *TOWIE* cast members. You're in!'

I was off-the-scale excited. I'd watched celebrities like Laurence Fox and Vogue Williams on *Bear Grylls: Mission Survive* drinking warm wee and crossing ravines on two pieces of rope, and now I couldn't wait for my turn to take on the challenge.

The producers were obsessive about keeping details of the show under wraps, so even the celebrities were kept in the dark about who else was taking part. The only name I managed to tease out of Shine TV was *Made in Chelsea*'s Ollie Locke. We'd met a few times at various TV events, and when I called him to spill the beans we set to work to discover the rest of the lineup.

Through various sneaky means at our vaccination and eye test appointments, between us we managed to find out that Aston Merrygold from JLS , the comedian Dom Joly, Dr Dawn Harper and former Labour councillor Karen Danczuk were also on board.

> **❝ I COULDN'T WAIT FOR MY TURN TO TAKE ON THE CHALLENGE ❞**

By Saturday 6 February, with the celebrities travelling in two separate groups to Panama from London Heathrow, myself and Ollie had worked out the rest of the lineup and they were: former *Blue Peter* presenter Zoe Salmon, ex rugby player and model Thom Evans, Mark Jenkins from Channel 4's *The Hotel* and comedian Josie Long. We also met the four TV producers who would be with us filming the whole experience – Vari, Jo, Ali and a guy called Tom who had previously worked on *TOWIE*.

From the get-go I was the best of buds with Ollie and Karen, and the same goes for Josie who was the most positive ray of sunshine I'd ever met in my life. I wasn't as close to Mark (we're from different worlds and different eras).

Before heading to the island we had to complete a two-day wilderness-survival course run by two SAS guys, who taught us things like how to kill an alligator, plants that can kill, and how to build a fire without matches.

We arrived on the island with nothing – just the clothes on our backs, a two-day supply of water, two machetes, two knives and filming equipment. I couldn't imagine how I was going to cope without my iPhone, toothbrush and memory-foam pillow. But there were no luxury items – this was no *I'm A Celebrity . . . !*

✺ Castaways ✺

On the first night we slept on the beach, which was a stupid decision because as the light faded millions of hermit crabs scuttled out of tiny holes in the sand and suddenly the beach was moving! Then in the early hours the tide came in and drenched us. I didn't sleep a wink.

'That was such a bad night's sleep,' yawned Dom the following morning.

'What?!' I yelled. 'You slept brilliantly! My ears are still ringing from the sound of your deafening all-night snoring.'

But not even Dom's night grunts could match the agony we felt inside our empty bellies. By the end of day one we'd not eaten a thing, day two came and went without food, and then day three, four . . .

A part of me hoped that Shine had hidden emergency food parcels in the jungle, but no such luck. For eight days no food passed our lips. For eight days we trekked for miles trying to find our camp, fresh water and food. Everything we did took ages. Keeping just one fire stoked required one person collecting wood all day long. We couldn't find the yucca plant we'd learned about in training, our fish traps didn't work, and it really seemed like no animal life existed on the island. We felt like the most useless wilderness survivors ever!

In our SAS training we learned that humans can go for 60 days without food but only three without water, so by the third day, when we still hadn't found a source of fresh water, the situation was critical. We all feared the worst – being forced to leave the island.

Then on day four Ollie, the producer Ali and I hit the jackpot – a semi-stagnant pond! We'd trekked around the island for hours to find it, through jungle, up treacherous hills and through thick swamp. At one point we were scaling what we thought was a vegetation-covered hill, but it was actually a mammoth vine bush 10 feet off the ground. On the return journey our knees were trembling as we envisaged falling through the vines and breaking every bone in our bodies.

To drink the pond water we had to filter it, and I donated my double-padded bra to do it. For once in my life I was grateful for having small boobs!

But the water tasted disgusting so I drank the bare minimum, and partial dehydration quickly took its toll. One week into the challenge I caught a glimpse of my reflection in a camera lens and it freaked me out. My hair looked like straw and my emaciated face was full of lines because there was no fluid in my body. I looked about 50 years old!

Every night before bed we comforted and tortured ourselves with the 'How much would you pay for . . . ?' game, where we placed imaginary bids on fantasy items of food and drink. Ollie said he'd pay £1,000 for a can of Sprite, and I agreed to stump up £500 for one slice of Domino's pizza! By night three Aston couldn't take it anymore.

'Guys, we can't play this game! It's doing bad things to me.'

Those might not be his exact words but that was the gist of it. Aston's face was drained of any emotion and he looked weary and weak. The next day he quit.

I was devastated. Aston's a top bloke with the voice of an angel, and every night he would drown out Dom's snoring by singing old-school RnB love songs.

On day eight our famine ended when Mark caught a triggerfish using a fishing trap made from a hook, a plastic water bottle and some string.

'Yeeeeessssss!' we cheered. We only had two spoonfuls of fish each but it was incredible to chew and the tiny meal gave us a much-needed energy boost. Even if the fish tasted like rubber!

At times, the hunger and thirst made me hangry (FYI that's bad-tempered or irritable as a result of hunger), but I knew I had to keep up my PMA or risk pulling down the spirits of the group.

Bear Grylls had shared some good advice before we disembarked the boat onto the island.

'The real test isn't on your body but on your minds,' he'd explained, adding that to stay strong we needed to stay happy and grateful. 'Don't survive, thrive,' were his words. But not everyone had listened.

66 TO DRINK THE POND WATER WE HAD TO FILTER IT, AND I DONATED MY DOUBLE-PADDED BRA TO DO IT 99

A few days in, during a group trek to find base camp, I clocked that Zoe wasn't carrying any kit. Josie, meanwhile, was lugging a heavy camera and fell down hard into a ditch because she was so weak and disorientated. I saw red.

'People are getting exhausted, Zoe, you are going to have to take the camera for a bit,' I screeched.

Zoe said she'd been offering the whole time to carry the kit and that she thought the real reason I was angry was that I had a problem with her. I knew Zoe was finding the experience harder than the rest of us, so maybe I was being a little insensitive. I hate confrontation and felt sick and uneasy about the whole episode. I didn't want an atmosphere in the camp.

'Zoe, I'm sorry for flipping,' I said. 'I know you're not feeling well but I feel like we need to help each other out. We're all finding it tough.'

'I'm feeling really ill. I'm helping as much as I can but my body is so weak,' she responded. We agreed it wouldn't be normal if we weren't bickering and hugged it out, then all was forgotten.

Hook, line and stinker

There were no winners or losers on *Celebrity Island*, just those who survived and those who didn't. Thom Evans, easily the beefiest contestant, was in the latter category and was proof that physical strength is no match for mental muscle.

Thom threw in the towel four days after Aston quit. He wasn't coping with the starvation and had begun acting like a zombie. One night I was talking to him for two minutes and nothing was registering. Thom seemed delirious and, looking back, that was so dangerous.

The toughest day of all was on day nine when I was fishing in the sea with Josie and producer Jo and I got a hook stuck in my finger. 'Oh my God, I know what's coming!' I cried, remembering what we'd learned in training. A fish hook barb (the sharp arrow-shaped bit) cannot exit a body part the way it entered. The only way is to pierce the finger again and push the hook out in the direction it went in.

Dr Dawn came over and attempted to force the hook out, but the pain was excruciating.

'Aaaaarrgh!' I shrieked. Then Dr Dawn stopped.

'I've got bad news, Lydia. It's gone through your finger joint. If I push any further it could sever your nerve ending and you'll never have feeling in your knuckle again. I'm really sorry, you might have to leave the island to get proper medical treatment.'

I couldn't believe what I was hearing.

'No! I've not come this far to leave the island because of a fish hook in my finger,' I said. 'You've got to try and get it out!'

Dr Dawn looked at me with trepidation in her eyes. Then she began to push.

I screamed like there was no tomorrow.

'Aaaaarrgh! AAAARRRRRRGGGGH!'

In the end Dr Dawn and the safety team (who travelled over from the mainland) had to slit my finger and I've never been in so much agony. I thought my life was going to end.

That evening I was calling Dom 'Scott', slurring my words, and had the most agonising tingles up my arm. I was clearly in shock and took 24 hours to recover.

The most mind-blowing experience of my adventure came on the penultimate day – when I killed a common caiman, which at three metres long and with razor-sharp teeth looked every bit like a crocodile. Ollie stumbled across it at the swamp.

'Oh my God, look at THAT!' he whispered. After 13 days of starvation there was only one option – we had to kill it.

Ollie, Karen and I were elected do the honours and I was shaking like a leaf as Karen crept up behind the caiman, grabbed it by the tail and pulled it out of the swamp, as I leapt forward and clamped its mouth shut with a string noose. Finally, Ollie – a vision in head-to-toe pink – threw himself onto the caiman's back, then stabbed it in the back of the head. It was the most macho gay man moment I've ever witnessed in my life. It was also utterly barbaric.

One month earlier I'd made a New Year's resolution to become vegan like Beyoncé, and there I was killing a giant reptile to eat its flesh. How hypocritical was I?! But for the sake of our camp and my own health it had to be done. Nobody in the camp had eaten more than 1,000 calories in a fortnight and we desperately needed food. I have no regrets.

In Amsterdam with my best mate Aruna

10 tips for the trip of a lifetime

Whether it's a round-the-world gap year, a snap year (a shorter trip for the time-conscious) or a one-month escape, here are my golden rules for getting the best out of globetrotting.

1 Choose your destination carefully: With over 190 countries to pick from you must zone in on exactly where you're going and understand why you're travelling there. Is there an activity or a cause that inspires you, for example volunteering at an orphanage in China? Have you got a burning desire to see the east coast of Australia? Tap into what makes you tick. And don't attempt to over-travel. It's not possible to see 20 countries in six months. To get the best out of a destination opt for quality over quantity. Immerse yourself into the country and culture. Plot your trip on a map to get a realistic idea of distances.

2 The nitty-gritty: Think finances. Calculate how much cash you'll need to fund the trip by budgeting for the cost of flights, hostels, local transport and overland adventure tours – then allow for extra for fun and emergencies. Are you going to work during the trip (if so, pack your CV) or do you need to find an extra part-time job before you leave Britain to boost your savings? The more cash you have, the longer your trip can be and the more you can do. Finally, don't forget to check out your visa requirements, take out travel insurance and get all necessary vaccinations.

3 **Read up:** The Lonely Planet books are my first port of call when plotting my travels. They go 10 steps beyond your average tourist guides, with off-the-beaten-track suggestions for eating out, accommodation, places to party and what to see and do. Best of all are their itinerary suggestions, must-see edits that help you make the most of whistle-stops. My top tips are to never stay anywhere for less than two days, and to use your feet or a bike over public transport to properly explore.

4 ***Hola* to hostels:** Before I got the travelling bug I was a hostel snob. I envisaged dirty fleapits, sleeping in unclean bedding and sharing dormitories with sweaty strangers. How wrong I was. A few hostels I've stayed in were on par with a hotel and were a fraction of the price. But even if you can afford to live it up in swanky hotels my advice is DON'T. Travelling is not just about the places you visit but the people you meet along the way and hostels create conversation. Chatting to other backpackers often leads to sage advice about a fab restaurant, a suggestion for a night out, or even a friend for life! I use hostelworld. com, which has 33,000 hostels listed in 170 countries, with over eight million guest reviews to help pick where to stay. TripAdvisor.co.uk is also excellent for sussing out a hostel's reputation.

5 **Pack light:** By lightening your load you'll not only avoid extra baggage charges but you'll save your spine (and your sanity). My advice is to make a list of what you think you need and then halve it. You always need less than you think, and remember that you can do laundry when you're away. My last bit of advice is ban 'what if' from your vocabulary. Trust me, that triple-layered thermal fleece body warmer won't be necessary in Papua New Guinea!

6 **Don't over-plan:** Reserving accommodation in advance is cheaper than turning up on the hoof, but I recommend only booking a hostel for the first night or two in a new city. Don't be too tied to an itinerary. Travelling is about being spontaneous and flexible, so move on early if you're not feeling the love for a place, stay longer if you are, and don't feel guilty if you're so hung-over from an impromptu night out that you sack off the mountain biking trek you've booked. Go with the flow!

7 **Be brave:** Sign up for a sky dive at sunrise, order deep-fried crocodile, book a night in a rainforest treehouse. Travelling is about living, so say yes to everything! It's why I ended up sleeping on a palm leaf on a desert island in Panama and living with a mountain community in Thailand.

8 **Listen to your gut:** If something doesn't feel right, don't do it. If you're not happy, change what's not making you happy. If you're struggling with the lack of privacy in a hostel, spoil yourself by 'flashpacking' in a hotel for a night or two. Georgia and I did this a couple of times when we were too hungover to talk to people! In Bangkok we stayed in a beautiful place called the Khaosan Palace so we could recharge. Remember, this is your trip. Make it perfectly yours.

9 **Pleasant distraction:** Travelling on a shoestring involves hours spent moving from A to B, be it by bus or by boat. I always pack a good book, play Candy Crush on my phone or read my Lonely Planet guide to keep myself entertained. Crossing the borders between Laos and Cambodia on my 2013 trip was the longest day of my life. Jill Mansell's novel *Head Over Heels* kept me sane.

10 **Safety catch:** Be wary of scammers and fraudsters but don't let the fear of being robbed or conned rule your trip. Most people are not out to harm you and the world isn't as dangerous as the news leads us to believe. Saying that, you must keep your wits about you and follow a few security rules: 1) Blend into your local environment by not dressing like a tourist (remove flash jewellery). 2) Keep your belongings on your body. My travelling day bag is not a designer leather tote but a cheap waterproof messenger satchel. 3) Use common sense, so don't get so drunk you have no control over what you're doing. 4) Use a Pacsafe bag protector – a steel wire net that covers your backpack and can be secured to something solid with a chain and padlock. 5) Give loved ones at home a copy of your itinerary, passport and travel insurance, in case you lose them.

✕ And finally . . .

~ Earplugs are your best friend.

~ Take an extra memory card for your camera.

~ Wear flip flops in the hostel shower.

~ Water, water, water. Without it you're no good for anything.

~ Fret not about Facebook. This is the one time of your life when you can disconnect from your phone.

The day we left the island by speedboat I saw myself in the mirror, and I was shocked. It was as if I was looking at a stranger – a skinnier stranger! I'd lost my bust, I could see the outline of my ribcage and I was covered in sandfly bites (I've still got the scars).

Celebrity Island was the hardest challenge of my life, but when it came to an end I couldn't stop the tears. I learned so much about myself, mostly that if you're mentally positive you can achieve anything.

At our hotel in Panama shortly before leaving to catch our flight back to London I had a conversation with Dom that I wish could have been bottled for ever.

'You've massively changed my perception of reality TV stars,' he admitted. 'Thank you.'

Wow. Not only had I survived *Celebrity Island*, but I'd shown that there's more to me than meets the eye, and I truly hope that when the show aired on television viewers felt the same.

66 THERE'S MORE TO EVERY HUMAN BEING THAN MEETS THE EYE. IT'S JUST A CASE OF TAKING THE TIME TO LOOK . . . 99

People say that other people's opinions don't matter but I disagree. When you're showing yourself in a positive light it should matter!

Dom and I were both guilty of judging books by their covers. He let his preconceptions about me rule initially, and I took him at face value. It was only when we invested time in getting to know each other that we discovered the true person and liked what we saw. The moment we really clicked was a couple of days into the challenge when I volunteered for the second day running to go on a big hike to look for food, water and shelter. I guess Dom started to realise how strong I was. I now love Dom to bits and since the show he's even written me into a new *Trigger Happy TV* sketch!

There's a saying by French writer and aviator Antoine de Saint-Exupéry: 'It is only with the heart that one can see rightly; what is essential is invisible to the eyes.' On *Celebrity Island* I learned to not only look with my eyes but with my heart, because there's more to every human being than meets the eye. It's just a case of taking the time to look . . .

🌹 *Vive la France!* 🌹

When I was a kid Mum, who's travelled around Europe, Central America and South America, would often preach to me about how important it was to visit different countries and soak up alternative cultures. She enrolled Georgia and me into an international school so that we could mix with kids from other backgrounds, learn French, German and Russian, and travel abroad. We often embarked on student exchanges as part of our school curriculum and my favourite one, in Year 8, was a one-week trip to France where I stayed with a girl called Mariah and her family.

I was so nervous. I'd only been learning French for just over a year and I was scared about living with a foreign family, but it ended up being a dream trip because I embraced the experience and immersed myself into the new culture. I remember thinking how androgynous the French girls were compared to us lot from Essex. They went to school in baggy trousers, trainers and hoodies and carried rucksacks, while us English girls were swanning around carrying trendy bowling bags and wearing skinny jeans and tops with designer names plastered across them (this was fashionable at the time!).

On the first day I got a rollicking from the head teacher when I pulled out my pink lipgloss during his welcome speech for a quick touch up. 'No make-up at this school!' he hollered,

The essence
of pleasure is
spontaneity

(Germaine Greer)

snatching the gloss out of my hand. I went bright red and for the rest of the trip my make-up stayed locked away.

But my interest in the big wide world started even earlier than that. As a six-year-old I remember clutching a rag doll that Mum brought me back from an Amish village during one of her trips to Ohio, where she was studying for her diploma in social work. I remember thinking: 'You'd never get this from a shop in England. I'd love to see this crazy other world.'

And that's what I'm doing. Since joining *TOWIE* I've visited some incredible, far-flung places to complete some insane fundraising challenges. And it's all thanks to Denise van Outen . . .

I first met Denise, who's a close pal of my manager Kirsty, at a celebrity party in 2011. She bounded over, all blonde hair and gorgeous tan, wearing an ear-to-ear smile, then paid me the biggest compliment.

'Lydia, you're doing so well on *TOWIE*. I just had to come and say hello,' she said, touching my arm affectionately. I was instantly star-struck. I'd watched Denise on Channel 4's morning TV show *The Big Breakfast* and seen her in glossy magazines. In Essex, celebrities don't come much bigger than Denise (okay, maybe David Beckham – but only just!) so I was bowled over . . . and a bit bamboozled.

'I've just started out on a reality show – I'm a Z-lister,' I thought. 'Why's this massive celebrity giving me the time of day?'

But as time went by it started to make sense. Very simply, Denise has the warmest heart, and I think she saw a bit of her younger self in me.

A week after the party Denise invited me to join her and Kirsty on a 300-mile bike trek across India. So in April 2012 I was bound for India with DVO, clutching a backpack and with big dreams of adventure in my heart . . .

🌹 On yer bike! 🌹

Our leg-burning nine-day cycling challenge across Rajasthan was in aid of London's Great Ormond Street Hospital, where my younger cousin Billy was treated as a baby after contracting a rare eye disease. The daughter of one of Denise's closest friends sadly passed away there, so it was a place that meant a lot to both of us.

Our Indian adventure began in New Delhi on the eve of the Hindu festival Holi, also known as the festival of colours. As we bombed around Old Delhi in a rickshaw, excitable local children raced after us throwing water bombs. It was amazing!

The following day, after catching a train to Agra (home of the Taj Mahal) we threw ourselves into Holi festival celebrations, barely stepping out of our hotel before being showered in gloriously coloured powders.

The cycling began on day three, and the first thing I noticed as we pedalled through villages and towns were the smells. Fabulous: rich spices and fragrant flowers. Foul: Burning dung cakes, which locals cooked food on, and raw sewage, which flowed beside every road.

I spent the majority of the trip chewing the ears off our two Indian guides, Vineet and Vaibhav. When I'm travelling I'm like an information Dyson, sucking up every detail about the country, from its history and politics to celebrities and sport.

We attracted attention everywhere we cycled because I don't think some locals had seen Westerners before, and with our pale skin and blonde hair, Denise, Kirsty and I stood out even more.

But on day five, as we cycled through a rural village in the direction of Bollywood-style pop music, nothing could have prepared us for the impact we made.

The music was in celebration of a real Indian wedding, where every member of the community seemed to be out in force, joining in the celebrations, and I was buzzing to see such a spectacle.

'This is amazing!' I yelled to Denise, who was cycling just a few feet ahead of me. Then I took one hand off my handlebars to do the 'screwing the light bulb' dance, made famous in the film *Bend It Like Beckham*, and momentarily lost control. My front wheel clipped Denise's back wheel and suddenly she was skidding and sliding all over the road before flying underneath a parked lorry.

'Denise! Oh my God, are you okay?' I screeched as Denise crawled out from beneath the truck in front of a gaggle of wedding guests.

But she didn't reply. Denise's face was a bright shade of red, so she was either embarrassed or utterly furious with me. I didn't know whether to roar with laughter or start a grovelling apology.

Denise clambered onto her bike and disappeared down the road faster than Laura Trott (now Kenny) in Rio 2016, as Kirsty, our guides and I raced behind, profusely apologising to the bemused wedding guests as we fled.

A mile down the road Denise stopped, took off her crash helmet and, in a deadly-serious tone, said: 'Well, that's it, let's just bloody call ourselves the wedding crashers!'

With that we collapsed into hysterical laughter.

Wherever we go in the world, daredevil Denise has some sort of near-death experience. A couple of years after our trip to India we were cycling across Vietnam (more of this later), and she careered into the side of a bridge, catapulted over her handlebars and nearly landed in the river.

But thank God for those moments. Charity challenges need to be challenging otherwise who the hell would sponsor us? It's not supposed to be a walk (or should I say cycle) in the park!

News of the wedding crashers spread swiftly across India and within days we had been invited to Karauli by Rajasthan's maharaja (that's the king to you and me). The place we stayed in was no Buckingham Palace . . . just like the building in the movie *The Best Exotic Marigold Hotel*, it was exquisite but in desperate need of a *Homes Under the Hammer* renovation, and as we wandered through the dusty, sometimes crumbling corridors, I could only imagine how stunning it must have been in years gone by – Princess Diana was once a visitor and rode in the family's vintage Rolls-Royce, which is still parked in the palace garage alongside a fleet of beautiful classic motors.

In one village we stopped to hand out gifts to some schoolchildren who were walking barefoot along the dusty road. As we handed out colouring crayons, balloons and tubes of bubbles, more children emerged, and the kids who already had goodies began sharing them out. Our gifts were probably their only possessions but they were happy to give them away. It reminded me why we were doing the challenge – to help British children less fortunate than ourselves.

That trip raised £35,000 for Great Ormond Street Hospital, and when I returned to England I vowed to do a charity challenge every year. I've since completed five challenges (more on these later) and I've got one person to thank for opening my eyes to a world where adventure meets altruism. I owe you one, Denise . . .

Back to basics

Since our late teens Georgia and I dreamed of travelling together, but once I joined *TOWIE* and then Bella Sorella became our joint baby, there was never a good time to escape.

As Christmas 2013 approached I thought: 'If we don't do this now, we never will.' So I threw caution to the wind and surprised Georgia on her birthday in November by telling her I'd planned a trip of a lifetime around Southeast Asia. On Boxing Day we flew to Kuala Lumpur, the capital of Malaysia, nursing horrendous Christmas Day hangovers, and spent two days exploring the city before flying to Thailand's Koh Samui island and catching a boat to Koh Pha Ngan for its legendary Full Moon Party. Just over a week later we moved on to Chiang Mai, a more mountainous, rural area of northern Thailand for a culture fix.

On the first night we spotted a notice in our hostel advertising an expedition to spend five days with a Thai community in the mountains, and Georgia and I shared the same thought: 'Let's go for it.'

The following morning, before sunrise, we grabbed our backpacks and boarded a minibus with nine other eager adventurers. Among the other guests were a couple of dreadlocked German guys, a Canadian couple with matching six-packs and a hilarious British couple called Johnny and Laura.

Following a gruelling eight-hour trek we arrived at a village where there was no electricity, no running water and – worst of all – no toilets. If you're wondering, we made do with a hole in the ground, and this was far from ideal given our diet staple in Thailand was curry, curry and more curry!

By day we busied ourselves with activities including white water rafting, jungle trekking, and cooking curries with the elder women, using recipes passed down from generation to generation. Evenings were spent huddled by the fire singing songs by Oasis and the Lighthouse Family with our tour guide, who we nicknamed Mr Chow because he looked and acted exactly like the character in *The Hangover*!

Night time, when temperatures plummeted to freezing, was particularly challenging. I hate the cold and have rubbish circulation, so I'm always Baltic. Sleeping on the floor of a wooden shack cushioned only by a rubber mattress and covered with a scratchy woollen blanket made for a mighty miserable night! I hadn't packed any warm clothes and was so frozen that I abandoned the hut to snuggle up with the village's Bangkaew dogs in front of the fire. My outdoor den was also welcome respite from the deafening snores of our German travelling companions!

You might think Georgia and I were bonkers for enduring hardship on our 'trip of a lifetime', but although the experience was tough it was also life-enhancing. In a five-star hotel you know what you're getting, and where's the fun in sunbathing, eating and drinking on repeat? I enjoy being pushed out of my comfort zone, meeting new people and creating amazing stories to tell my grandkids.

One morning, mesmerised by the sun rising over the mountain top, I had a panicked thought: 'There's so much of the world to see. What happens if I don't manage to fit it all in?'

By the time I'm 30 I plan to have visited 20 per cent of the world. I even have an app on my phone called Been, where you can work out how much of the world you've yet to visit. Right now I've visited 13 per cent – so seven per cent to go before I've hit my target!

After our mountain community adventure Georgia and I journeyed through the sleepy country of Laos and on to Cambodia, where I fell in love with the people and the place. We met some truly special people, all of whom I'm still in touch with to this day. I pledged to return as soon as possible, and within a year that promise was fulfilled . . .

🌹 The boy who broke my heart 🌹

Cambodia is my favourite place in the whole world. Fact. I came to this conclusion the second time I visited, in January 2015, when I joined Denise, Kirsty and our good friends, the television presenters Matt Johnson and Zoe Hardman on a 372-mile bike ride through Vietnam and Cambodia. We did it to raise money for mental health charity Mind, for which Matt's an ambassador, and the Vipingo Village Fund – a charity set up by Zoe's parents in 2006 to help Aids-affected children in the village of Vipingo just north of Mombasa in Kenya. Sadly, Zoe's dad, Peter, died in the summer of 2013 so her mum, Carol, now runs the organisation single-handedly.

I'm passionate about Cambodia's culture and history. The people have been through so much, enduring an awful civil war in the 1960s and 70s, including mass genocide at the hands of the brutal Khmer Rouge government. Under the leadership of Marxist Pol Pot, the army wiped out nearly two million people, millions of city folk were forced to work on communal farms in the countryside, and whole families died from starvation, disease, overwork or execution. It was the stuff of a real-life horror film and it wasn't until 1992, when the United Nations intervened, that civil rule and order were restored.

Our journey started in Vietnam's Ho Chi Minh City and finished in Cambodia's Siem Reap, taking us through beautiful rural villages, including one in the Kampong Thom province where we met an 81-year-old man who'd lost lots of his family during the Khmer Rouge regime. He didn't speak any English but our tour guide Peah translated his eye-opening stories. It was fascinating for us and he enjoyed it too (I suspect he gets very lonely).

Everywhere we went children waved and elders blessed us. In Cambodia the spirituality and positivity of the people is as beautiful as its landscape.

'The Cambodian people have been through so much horror and heartbreak, so how come they're always smiling and so humble?' I asked Peah, as we cycled through a sea of smiling faces in another village.

'It's because you are our heroes,' he smiled. 'The Western world saved Cambodia from civil war and poverty and the people regard anyone from the West who visits as their saviour.'

Then Peah told me about his brother who is living with Aids.

'My brother would be dead if it wasn't for you. The West set up three hospitals in Cambodia, which now provide free healthcare for children, educate people about sexual health, and medicate those with HIV and Aids.'

Peah invited us to meet his family and within minutes of arriving in the village word of us spread. Soon children were hanging off us, and as we handed out gifts, just as we had in India, they giggled and smiled.

I took a shine to a three-year-old boy and Peah explained that he was one of three orphaned brothers.

'Their mum ran away when they were young because their dad was a heavy drinker. Eventually he abandoned them too so they live with their elderly grandad. Unfortunately he's poor so it's up to the village to support them financially.'

The story broke our hearts. All I could think was: 'That poor grandad.'

I turned to Denise. 'That poor man, trying to support three young children.'

'We've got to give him money,' said Denise. 'How much do you have on you?'

We opened our zip pockets, where we only held a small amount of money for emergencies, and we scraped together $60, which wasn't a great deal to us but was enough to feed the grandad and his boys for a month.

They lived in a one-room shack on poles, accessible only by a ladder, and when we handed over the money the grandad started to weep.

'Thank you,' he said, using Peah to translate. 'I've never known such kindness from strangers.'

It was the smallest contribution I've ever made in my life but it was the most impactful because I could instantly see how my money was making a difference.

Charity should always be personal to you in some way. Take my younger brother Freddie. He was diagnosed with juvenile epilepsy just before his seventeenth birthday in June 2015, following his first fit. He's had ten seizures since but thankfully I've never seen him have one. I'm not sure I could handle watching him lose control like that. Through a future charity challenge I want to fund research into epilepsy, so other children don't have to experience what Freddie's going through.

🌹 Climbing for CoppaFeel! 🌹

When *The Sun on Sunday*'s *Fabulous* magazine approached me and my *TOWIE* castmate Ferne McCann to lead a team of readers to the ancient mountain city of Machu Picchu in Peru on a ten-day trek in aid of breast cancer charity CoppaFeel! I didn't hesitate to say yes.

Machu Picchu – one of the New7Wonders of the World – was on my must-visit list but, more importantly, I'd seen CoppaFeel!'s founder, Kris Hallenga, in a television documentary a couple of years earlier, and had felt hugely inspired by her spirit.

Eight years ago doctors failed to spot Kris's breast cancer and dismissed a lump in her breast as hormonal. By the time she was diagnosed in 2009 at the age of 23 the disease had spread to her spine. It's now terminal, so for Kris the future is uncertain – but by no means bleak.

Instead of curling up and giving up when she was diagnosed, Kris set up CoppaFeel!, which now raises more than £1 million a year and encourages women and men to check their breasts. Each month the charity sends over 30,000 boob-check text reminders, and every year they tour 65 universities and 10 festivals. There are also 90 volunteers, called Boobettes, who tour the country sharing their breast cancer stories. Talk about inspiring.

Ferne and I could spread the message to young female *TOWIE* fans, which was a big pull to sign up, as was knowing that my beloved Nanny Doll had had a double mastectomy and beaten breast cancer after early detection in the 1940s. Did you know that in the UK nearly 60,000 people are diagnosed with breast cancer every year? That's the equivalent of one person every 10 minutes. The statistics are frightening.

'How can we raise big money for CoppaFeel! without just asking people to sponsor us?' Ferne and I pondered over a glass of wine one night after filming *TOWIE*.

'What about a sponsored walk, a tea morning or a bring-and-buy sale?' suggested Ferne.

'No, let's go BIG,' I said. 'Let's have a ball!'

We couldn't have wished for more support from friends, family and *TOWIE* cast members when we threw the Boob Summer Ball on 2 August 2015. We arranged live singers, a performance from the Dreamboys for the ladies, and a raffle with over 20 prizes including spa breaks and flight tickets. The night raised £9,000.

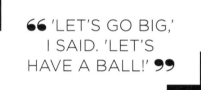

66 'LET'S GO BIG,' I SAID. 'LET'S HAVE A BALL!' 99

Flying to Peru was intense. We caught three flights over 15 hours, and when we landed the effect of the country's 2,000-metre altitude was instant. Some of the team had nausea, another had a nosebleed, and I felt like I'd run a marathon.

'How on earth am I going to walk up to eight hours a day for ten days to Machu Picchu breathing this air?!' I said to Ferne, clutching my chest as we waited for our rucksacks in the baggage hall. I'm not a fantastic breather at the best of times because of my sinuses, so I knew it was going to be a real struggle.

Luckily, we had two days to acclimatise. The following day we clocked up a five-hour trek along the Pikillaqta ruins, where we stopped at a deserted shrine to watch a group of Andean people perform a spiritual ceremony called a Quitu blessing. They invited us to share their holy bread and corn from the sacred mountains, and we made wishes on coca leaves then buried them under a rock formation. I remember wishing good health to my family and friends. It was quite soon after Freddie had been diagnosed with epilepsy, and I got a bit teary as I prayed for it to not stop him from achieving his dreams. I also prayed that Arg would stay on the straight and narrow and for us to have a happy future together.

As we set off from the village of Cancan in the Lares Valley I remember thinking that a walking trek would be a breeze compared to cycling in 90-degree Indian sunshine. How wrong I was. Within two hours I was nursing a nosebleed, panting and wondering: 'What have I signed up for?'

Altitude sickness – when a decrease in atmospheric pressure and oxygen makes breathing difficult – hit me like a truck on day four. I was delirious and hallucinating.

But the hardest part of the trek was dealing with the cold. When you see Machu Picchu in photographs it's usually bathed in beautiful sunshine, but during our visit it snowed, rained, hailed and was permanently freezing. I wore thermals, fleece pyjamas, a jumper, a bobble hat and two pairs of socks, but when temperatures dropped to -4°C I was beside myself. I was so cold that I wore the same pair of knickers for a week because I couldn't bear to take off my clothes to baby-wipe myself clean! Gross!

Machu Picchu was one of my toughest challenges to date because I felt the most mentally weak. Being cut off from my family (no phone signal) and the hell of altitude sickness and coldness was bad enough. But one evening I accidentally flooded my tent with water from my drinking bottle, so I was damp the whole night. I cried myself to sleep thinking about how much I missed home, my warm bed, my family.

But there's a quote by Bob Marley that goes: 'You never know how strong you are until being strong is the only choice you have.' And I only had to glance around the group of incredible women (and one man) in Team Machu Picchu to realise the truth in that.

On our final day, after climbing nearly 2,000 steps to the summit of Machu Picchu Mountain, we returned to the Pikillaqta ruins, where one trekker, a 36-year-old woman called Lucy Culkin, scattered the ashes of her cousin Mandy who had died of breast cancer two years earlier. Mandy was just 29.

'I want to leave them somewhere as beautiful and magical as my cousin was,' said Lucy, her face full of pride, sadness and hope. My heart splintered as I imagined the pain that Mandy's family had been through. I'd been devastated when my Grandad Lou died, but I felt comfort knowing he'd had a good life. For a young woman's flame to burn out at 29 seemed cruel and unfair. In a moment my frustrations over altitude sickness, cold nights and my damp groundsheet evaporated. All I could think was: 'Thank God I'm helping to raise awareness and money to fight this vile disease.' On that trip Team Machu Picchu raised over £58,000 for CoppaFeel! and I'm so incredibly proud of that achievement.

During my GCSEs and A levels I struggled to keep a lid on my anxiety, and when I started on *TOWIE* the stress of arguing with James took its toll on my body, as I've talked about earlier. I've always been a worrier and prone to panicking, but since exploring the world I now have more perspective and feel less stressed.

We're all guilty of getting unnecessarily overwhelmed by life's challenges, and during those times we have two choices: stress and worry and let it consume us or smile and get on with it. These days I no longer get sucked into the drama and bitchiness on *TOWIE* and I handle negative emotions more healthily by overpowering them with positivity. Seeing the world through the eyes of those less fortunate than me has given me balance and perspective. And that's priceless.

The world's your oyster

I've travelled far and wide but have whittled down my favourite places ever to count on one hand. Don't forget to tweet me when you get there! #LydiasTopFive

1 **Leigh-on-Sea, Essex.** I'm an Essex patriot. Not only has it been my home for most of my life, it also forged me a career. Essex is HUGE. People don't realise how much there is to see, and some parts are truly stunning, like Leigh-on-Sea – a beautiful seaside town, about an hour from where I live in Buckhurst Hill. The promenade is lined with cute vintage boutiques and chintzy cafes and the fish and chips are to die for, followed by ice cream from the awesome Poco Gelato.

2 **Loreto, Italy.** This is where my grandad was born and lived for many years, and lots of my family members still reside here. A church called Basilica della Santa Casa is a beautiful centrepiece to the town, and inside is a tiny house where locals believe the Virgin Mary once lived. My family is Roman Catholic and very religious, so visiting the basilica is a ritual every time I go to Loreto. When you enter the sleepy town it's like stepping back in time. Nuns and monks sit in the piazzas, there are ice-cream parlours selling pistachio and stracciatella ice cream, and old women sell rosary beads. It is very magical and so Italian.

3 **Brick Lane, east London.** One of my top places to visit in London. In the heart of trendy Shoreditch the area is home to some of my favourite vintage stores, including Beyond Retro, and the street is lined with the best curry houses and the ever-so famous Jewish bagel shop Beigel Bake, which sells the world's most mouthwatering smoked salmon, cream cheese and salt beef bagels. It's open 24 hours a day so I've made many taxi detours here after nights out in London! Most of all, I love how individuality is celebrated in Shoreditch and nobody fits a mould.

4 **Gili Trawangan, Indonesia.** When travelling through south-east Asia in 2013 my sister and I made some friends for life. One of them was a south Londoner called Cheryl who eventually fulfilled her dream of becoming a scuba-diving instructor on an island called Gili Trawangan in Indonesia. Two weeks after I broke up with Arg in March 2016 I found out that he'd been planning to propose to me on the holiday we had booked to the Caribbean. The thought of staying in England during that time with a head full of 'what ifs' made me so sad. So when Cheryl invited me to visit her on Gili Trawangan I practically bit her hand off. I spent two weeks diving for turtles, island hopping between Gili Air, Gili Meno and Lombok, and sipping on fresh fruit smoothies. Nights were spent at our favourite bar, Ombak, owned by a guy called Herianto who was born and bred on the island. I couldn't believe how chilled and laidback their lives were. Gili Trawangan is a place to visit when you need to switch off from the world and fall in love with yourself again.

5 **Cambodia.** I've spoken a lot about this country and I often encourage friends to go. Frankly, I should work for the tourist board! Cambodia has a brutal but eye-opening history, is full of bustling cities, paradise islands and the most humble souls. One of my favourite places in this enchanting country is Siem Reap, which is home to Angkor Wat, a construction of Hindu temples from the 12th century. You could spend a week visiting every building, but I would suggest hiring a local tuktuk driver with good English for a day to show you the main points of interest. The sites are out of this world, and if you're a fan of *Lara Croft: Tomb Raider* you have to visit, as part of the movie was filmed here. Siem Reap is also bursting with nightlife, mainly found on the famous pub street and the Angkor What? bar is a must for an all-singing, all-dancing night out with the best drink buckets in town. Remember to sign the graffiti walls and look out for my name! My favourite restaurant in there is called Genevieve's on Sok San Road in the Wat Damnak area. It's run by a German couple who employ local orphans and teach them the hospitality business. When we were there for my 23rd birthday one worker – a teenage orphan who had his face burnt in a house fire – sang all night for us. We later found out he was a contestant on the Cambodian equivalent of *The X Factor*!

The island of Koh Rong is a slice of Cambodian paradise and the country's best-kept secret – a place with no cars, no electricity after 8 p.m. and only four small villages. We spent days chilling on giant beanbags and barbecuing freshly caught fish.

There's an old Chinese proverb that goes: 'Enjoy yourself. It's later than you think.' I couldn't agree more with this sentiment. We only have one life so it's important that we use the time we have left wisely and fill it to the brim with experiences and memories. So take a pen and paper and make your own list of countries that you want to visit, and make those dream trips happen. And don't forget to send me a postcard!

#8
THE FUTURE'S BRIGHT

WHEN I FIRST STARTED THINKING ABOUT
THE CONTENT OF THIS BOOK I MADE NOTES
ABOUT WHAT I MIGHT INCLUDE IN EACH
CHAPTER. FOR THIS ONE, WHERE I LOOK
FORWARD TO THE FUTURE, I WROTE:
'MARRIAGE AND BABIES WITH JAMES
ARGENT.' ISN'T IT FUNNY HOW LIFE PLANS
CAN CHANGE IN A HEARTBEAT?

F our months passed before James and I came face to face,
following our big split in March 2016. Any couple in the
normal world would never see or speak to each other after
going their separate ways. No such luck on planet *TOWIE*.

When two cast members split or have an argument a 'bump in'
scene – where the two people randomly bump into each other
and talk – always follows. To the viewers this scene seems like a
pure coincidence but in reality it's a carefully planned moment
orchestrated by *TOWIE* producers. In the early days I would never
know when a 'bump in' was coming so it would catch me
unaware. I've since learned to expect the unexpected, and I've
accepted that it's my duty to lay bare my feelings in this very
awkward situation, no matter how tough it feels on my heart.

To celebrate the start of summer and series 18 the cast flew out
to Spain to film a one-off special called *The Only Way Is Mallorca*.
Everyone was buzzing about it. Ten days of sun, sea, sand and
sangria – all in the name of work. How lucky were we?

I earned my pay packet in episode one. Three days into the trip
I was strolling along the shore chatting with Chloe Lewis when I
spotted James walking towards us. The 'bump in' was happening
and my stomach was doing back-flips with nerves and adrenaline.

'How are you?' said James, casting his eyes to the sand after

Chloe made her excuses. It was so obvious he was nervous and I instantly regretted drinking heavily the night before because the hangover was making me anxious. Not that I showed it.

'Good now,' I replied. James smiled. I didn't.

James told me I looked 'insane', said he was sorry and that he 'absolutely adores' me. Then I let rip.

'When I look at you I'm angry but I feel really sad for you. You had everything that you ever wanted. You got me back after all those years. We were getting a house, we were getting engaged but nothing was ever enough for you. I tried to support you and hold your hand through life. I gave you everything. You made me hate you. You are so selfish and you will only ever care about yourself. You've never supported me through life. My whole life was invested in you and yet you still let me down. I deeply don't want us to ever be friends. You're not the kind of person that I would want in my life. I would like you to stay away from my friends and family. My life is my life now and I'm getting on with it. We'll just keep it that we're strangers. We'll just walk past each other, and that's how I would like it. I don't want to know you anymore. Okay?'

I didn't give James a chance to reply. I walked past him and with every footstep I made in the beautiful golden sand I felt stronger and stronger. I could hear James gently sobbing behind me and they were tears of regret, shame and frustration. James had let me down for years, constantly promising to change and fix his problems. All that time I'd compromised my own wants, morals, needs and feelings, but not anymore. On that beach I yanked back control, self-esteem and pride, and my strength seemed to disable James. For the first time he seemed weaker than I'd ever felt.

Later that night, for the first time in months, I cried. I felt sad that I no longer knew the man I'd been preparing to buy a house with and marry. It was an emotional time.

The next time I saw James was at Bobby's Big Top birthday party at the end of series 18. I told him that I didn't want us to feel like we had to run away from each other anymore, because although I'm still hurt, I'm not as angry now as I was then. The reality is that we'll still have to see each other when filming and I'm not the sort of person who likes tension hanging over me. Sometimes you just have to be the bigger person and put the past to bed.

Apart from a moment of weakness out in Marbella (cough, cough), I've not really seen him since, but we've messaged each other on special occasions like birthdays and Christmas to wish each other well. Just after it was announced ithat I was appearing on Channel 4's *The Jump*, James called.

'I wish you'd told me you were doing the show before I read it in the press,' he said.

'We don't speak very often, James. I didn't think to call you,' I said. It was true. Calling James about every little development in my life was our old modus operandi. But no more.

'I'm really happy for you,' continued James. 'But promise me one thing. When you take part in the Skeleton please can I be the first person you call?'

The Skeleton is a terrifying race that involves flying face-first onto a heavy metal sled, then hurtling down a twisting ice track. Before I did it I was so petrified I cried my eyes out and threw up, so afterwards, when I got back to the hotel, I messaged James to tell him. He was the only person from back home that understood my ordeal so we ended up having a bit of a laugh about it.

I can honestly say I'm not attracted to James any more, but – although I like the thought of completely cutting away from him – I can't because I still worry about him. When he's going through a tough time in his personal life, I'll always be there to help. I can't switch off that side of me that cares.

It is good
to have an end
to journey
towards, but
it is the journey
that matters
in the end
(Ursula Le Guin)

🌀 First comes love 🌀

I'm a hopeless romantic, I wear my heart on my sleeve, and I know there's someone out there for me so I'm confident I'll fall in love again in the not-too-distant future. Before *The Jump* a couple of guys were on the scene – I went on a couple of dates with a guy who I met at the London ME hotel and things got a bit more serious with a construction business owner I met there too. With the latter, I knew things would never be more than physical. He was a bit of a player so I wasn't sad when things fizzled out after two months. But I enjoyed it while it lasted!

Whoever I choose to marry, my wedding dress will be the same. When my Nanny Maureen married my Grandad Lou in St Peter's Italian church in Clerkenwell, central London in 1957, she wore a wedding dress similar to the Pierre Balmain number that Audrey Hepburn chose for her 1954 wedding to Mel Ferrer – a beautiful white lace tea dress. The style truly takes my breath away because it's so classically elegant, and when it's my turn to walk down the aisle, I'll pay homage to my nan and wear exactly the same style.

I'm 26 and not planning to rush into making babies. Nowadays the average age for a woman to have a baby is 30, compared to 27 in 2004, so I'm not stressing about rushing things. Mum was 30 when she had me in 1991, and I once observed to her that she must have been considered unusual back then for waiting so long to get pregnant. 'Bloody hell! I'm not a dinosaur!' she replied. But I know that when the time comes I'll be a great mum. I'm very maternal and have had lots of practice, growing up in a fostering family and caring for my best friend and neighbour Danni's baby daughter, Summer-Rose. Mum tells me that my birth was super quick – she went into labour around midnight and I popped into the world a couple of hours later. I'm praying that this runs in the family and I deliver babies like Speedy Gonzales too!

The celebrity mum I most admire is Angelina Jolie. She allows her six kids to be individuals, teaches them not to conform to societal expectations, and leads by example to be charitable, which shows them the importance of giving. Like Angelina, my plan is to have lots of children – three or four at least – and I'm also considering fostering when the time is right. That's if my future husband wants the same thing. According to Banardo's another 8,600 foster carers are needed to provide loving homes for the 92,000 children who are currently in care in Britain. It's sad that children are suffering in our society, and the more I think about the difference that my parents made to so many kids' lives the more I feel inspired to do the same. I also won't have a baby or foster while I'm on *TOWIE*. Working in reality television is so unpredictable, as is motherhood, and whilst others on the show have managed it I don't think I could juggle the two. I'll need a slower-paced existence to feel comfortable bringing a baby into the world.

> **❝ I NEVER WANT TO BE FINANCIALLY DEPENDENT ON A MAN ❞**

When I was younger I assumed I'd have kids with a guy who earned enough money to allow me to be a stay-at-home mum. Well, I've got news – that's now my worst-case scenario! I don't judge women who give up work to have babies – everyone is different and each to their own – but I wouldn't feel satisfied if I sacrificed work for family. More importantly, I never want to be financially dependent on a man. I'm a fierce believer in equality in a relationship. Don't get me wrong, I love tradition and romance (what girl doesn't?), but being on a level pegging with my significant other is crucial to the health of the relationship.

At the beginning of last year, when James and I were still together and were house hunting, we fell in love with a derelict four-storey townhouse in east London. Our offer was accepted and we agreed to split the deposit between us and equally share the mortgage, despite our salaries being different. I've always earned good money but James's annual income was greater than mine as he was appearing in more things. I could have let James stump up the majority of the deposit (he offered, and I know plenty who would have accepted) but my pride wouldn't allow it.

When James and I broke up (on the day our offer on the house was accepted) I tried to find a way to fund the project alone, but the costs were too mammoth so I abandoned ship. Instead I invested in a property in trendy Hackney, east London. This won't be a new pad for myself but rather an investment, as my parents always encourage investing in bricks and mortar. For now, I'm staying put in my little house in Buckhurst Hill.

✿ House rules ✿

When I bought my two-up two-down cottage I was bursting with pride. I'd saved like a beast since joining *TOWIE*, squirrelling away all the money I could, and by 2012 I'd accumulated my deposit. If you're fortunate enough to get a foot on the property ladder my advice is to put your stamp on it – buy a renovation project and give it a big dose of TLC. Over the years I have invested in a new roof, boiler, flooring and a few cosmetic improvements. This has paid dividends because four years on my house value has nearly doubled!

After ploughing my savings into the deposit I was broke, so brand new furnishings had to wait. I didn't mind. Patience makes you appreciate what you eventually buy, and that's true whether you're buying a house, a handbag . . . or looking for the perfect man! Since James and I broke up I've splashed out on getting the garden fence replaced, installed some smart storage for the chimney breast coves, and invested in a purple crushed-velvet sofa – a little reminder to any guest that they're in a woman's home!

✹ Where I've come from, where I'm going ✹

I have to pinch myself when I look at how far I've come and think about everything I've achieved – my business, my fashion achievements, where I've travelled in the world, the parties I've been invited to and the people I've met. And I know I owe a huge part of those achievements to *TOWIE*. I will forever be grateful to the show for the opportunities it has given me. The cast and crew are like my family and I love going to work. The only time my name will disappear off the cast list is if I get handed my P45 or when *TOWIE* ends. Let's be honest. The first option ain't going to happen – I'm too much of a goody two-shoes to get myself fired! But when *TOWIE* reaches the finishing line it'll be the end of an amazing chapter, and life after will be a tough adjustment after all these years in the spotlight. But I hope I've never lost sight of what's real in my life. I have the same friends, I've never abandoned Essex to live in a swanky apartment in Knightsbridge (not that I could afford to anyway!) and I still hang out at the same places.

I hope to continue working in television and ideally that will include more fashion presenting. I'm also determined to develop a TV show to encourage people to foster and adopt. During my *TOWIE* break I developed an idea for a TV programme that would educate young people about important political matters like adoption. Kirsty secured me meetings with some key production companies. At the time of the meetings I felt super confident and like one of Alan Sugar's contestants on *The Apprentice*, but although the people I met seemed passionate about my idea they never invited me back. But I get it. It's a cut-throat industry. I can't expect to waltz in and have my first pitch commissioned.

As for my blog, it has an ever-growing reach so that will continue, and Bella Sorella will always be my baby!

My top three west Essex hangouts

1 Pizzeria Bel-Sit
439–441 High Rd, Woodford Green, Woodford, IG8 0XE

A famous Italian restaurant that has been in business since 1981. The food and atmosphere are brilliant and so traditional you feel like you're in a pizzeria in an old Italian town.

2 Robins Pie & Mash
14 High St, Wanstead, E11 2AJ

Server of old Cockney fayre and the best in the business. This place opened 80 years ago when Wanstead was part of Essex (it's officially in east London now, but many residents insist their address is 'Wanstead, Essex'). When I'm there I feel like the Kray twins could walk in at any minute. It's so old-school. The staff wear pinny aprons and hair nets and there are nostalgic black-and-white photos on the walls.

3 The Three Colts
54 Princes Rd, Buckhurst Hill, IG9 5EE

I had a part-time job here when I was 18. Now I live less than a two-minute walk away and I love popping in for a cheeky wine in the evening. My dad is in there most nights with his mates, and they're all in the building trade so I often pester them to do odd jobs around my house!

My 30 before 30 list

One of my best friends, Lauren, had a panic on her 29th birthday (as many girls do) and she started questioning if she had done enough in her life. With that, the 30 before 30 list was born! The rest of the girls and I vowed we'd make one too, and so on my 25th birthday I sat down to draw up the following list. I could afford to be a little more adventurous with my list as I have five years to achieve it. Here it is . . .

1 **Get rid of my verruca.** I've had the little bugger for years and have avoided getting it treated because my doctor says I can't wear heels for six weeks after. I'm not a fan of flats but medical needs must!

2 **Visit at least 20 per cent of the world.** The next places on my hit list are the Philippines and a safari in Africa.

3 **Go whale watching.** I've been obsessed with whales ever since watching *Blackfish*, the 2013 documentary about a performing killer whale called Tilikum. Iceland is among Europe's best whale-watching destinations so I'm planning to go there.

4 **Go to Glastonbury.** I've never been able to get tickets and I was particularly gutted to miss out in 2016 because I'm a huge Adele and Coldplay fan. I've heard it's a really spiritual place and the ultimate date in the festival diary. When I finally make it to Worthy Farm I know one thing – I won't be camping! I've slept in a tent in Peru and India but Glasto is too much of a mud-fest for me!

5 **Become fluent in Italian.** I can speak roughly 20 per cent of the language. I can order food in a restaurant and get by on holiday but I need to learn more. It's my heritage, my history and a mark of respect to my lovely Grandad Lou.

6 **Get a selfie with Sarah Jessica Parker.** I have to meet her, I just have to! Hopefully she'll read this book and get in touch! I'd even wait in the rain outside a movie premiere to get my picture taken with her.

7 **Do the *Sex and the City* tour in New York City.** I have been to New York twice: once with Tom Kilbey and another time with my family when I was 15. My dad hired a Cadillac and we spent three weeks driving from New York up to Vermont. The next time I go I'll pay homage to SJP on the *SATC* tour.

8 **Learn how to play golf.** This is what people do as they get older and I'm 26 now so it's time to get handy with some clubs. Nineteenth hole, anyone?

9 **See a top designer show at London Fashion Week.** Give me any seat, even on the back row and I'll be happy.

10 **Own a Dolce & Gabbana dress.** My favourite fashion house in the whole world, and although I own a couple of pairs of D&G shoes I've never justified spending money on a dress. One special day I'll treat myself!

11 **Stay a night in the Poseidon or Neptune underwater suites at Atlantis, The Palm hotel in Dubai.** I'm obsessed with fish and marine life and during a trip to Koh Lanta in Thailand I took the plunge and got my PADI Open Water Diver certification. Now I go scuba diving wherever I can.

12 **Run the London Marathon.** Or perhaps I should say 'complete the London Marathon'! I go along every year to cheer on the runners and always feel inspired to try it myself. I'm not the best runner, mainly due to the fact I fractured my ankle when I was 16 on a trampoline and it has never been quite the same. But one day I will bite the bullet and take the plunge.

13 **Visit all of the New7Wonders of the World.** In 2000 an initiative was launched to select the New7Wonders of the World, and the results of a public poll were announced in 2007. Apparently it's possible to visit them all for £5,194 and I've got three in the bag already: Machu Picchu in Peru, the Taj Mahal in India, and the Colosseum in Rome. Anyone fancy joining me on a voyage of discovery to visit the Great Wall of China, Petra in Jordan, the Chichén Itzá in Yucatán, Mexico, and Christ the Redeemer in Rio de Janeiro, Brazil?

14 **Go to Rio de Janeiro for carnival.** Free-spirited, bursting with colour, and fashion so creative it would put Vivienne Westwood to shame. Rio hosts the biggest carnival celebration in the world every spring and I need to be part of it!

15 **Volunteer for Crisis at Christmas.** Crisis is the national charity for single homeless people and every Christmas they need more than 11,000 volunteers, from 23–30 December, to help at their centres across the country.

16 **Stay in an igloo.** I'm on a mission to sleep in the coolest places . . . literally! I can't stand the cold but I want to tap in to my inner Eskimo. At the Kakslauttanen Arctic Resort in Finland you can watch the stars and the northern lights from your bed in a glass igloo, but that's cheating! At the Iglu Village in Kühtai in Austria you reside in actual snow igloos. Now we're talking . . .

17 **Volunteer at an animal sanctuary.** Working as a giant panda keeper in China, nursing distressed orphaned elephants in Thailand, or reintroducing sloths back into the wild in Costa Rica. Animals are one of my greatest passions and I'd love to spend some time making a difference to their lives.

18 **Visit Spain for the tomato-throwing festival.** La Tomatina happens every last Wednesday in August in a town called Buñol in Spain. For two hours locals and tourists pelt each other with 125,000 kilos of tomatoes. I'll save my white bikini for another day!

19 **Ride in a hot air balloon.** Potential future boyfriends take note . . .

20 **Get a TV show commissioned.** I want to create my own TV show, probably a documentary about fostering, and see it broadcast on one of the mainstream channels.

21 **Raise at least £100,000 for charity.** I've raised £47,190 so far and I am currently planning my next charity challenge adventure, to happen in November 2017.

The ones I've achieved:

22 **Meet a turtle.** When I was in Indonesia in March 2016 I told my scuba-diving friend Cheryl about my burning desire to meet a turtle. 'To me they look like friendly, old and wise creatures of the world,' I said to her one day over a watermelon smoothie. So the following day she took me diving at a place called Turtle Bay, which is sandwiched between Gili Trawangan and Lombok. Twenty minutes into the dive everyone was pointing at me. I looked around and saw an enormous two-foot turtle to my left. At first I was a little nervous but then came tears of happiness. It was such a magical moment. The world is truly so beautiful.

23 **Get a tattoo.** I've now got a fish hook tattooed on my left middle finger. It covers the scar from removing the fish hook when I was filming *Celebrity Island*. Don't worry Mum, my body isn't going to become a blank canvas for body art. I'll probably get a couple more on my fingers along my travels and that's it.

24 **Wine tasting.** I adore wine and on our family holiday to Sant Amico, Italy in August 2016 I went wine tasting with my mum, dad, brother and my parents' best friends Elaine and Paul. At the Antica Cantina Sant Amico we tried rosé, white, red and dessert wine and ended up in fits of laughter as we got more and more drunk. It was a beautiful, traditionally Italian afternoon!

25 **Sleep on a desert island.** Bear Grylls. Need I say more?

26 **Go inside Buckingham Palace.** I visited Lancaster House in March 2015 when Mum was awarded by Minister for Children and Families, Edward Timpson for her dedication to being a foster carer for over 20 years. Then in May 2016, after being announced as fostering ambassadors for the Department for Education, we were invited to Buckingham Palace for afternoon tea to celebrate 150 years of the Barnardo's charity. When we left we walked directly through the palace's Grand Entrance. It was truly magnificent and we felt fabulous. Hilariously, a group of Asian tourists who were taking photos spotted us and asked if we were royals. Mum and I replied 'Yes!' then laughed the whole way home.

29 **Buy a buy-to-let property.** After months of research on up-and-coming places to invest in, I settled on the idea of Hackney Wick in London. I arranged for a viewing of a new build, one-bed flat opposite the station and within close proximity to an area that will soon become a buzzy restaurant hot spot. It was the only flat I viewed but it was perfect, and I made the offer the next day. I exchanged in January 2017, and I feel very proud of this achievement.

27 **Holiday in Las Vegas with the girls.** I ticked this off my list in June 2016. And what happens in Vegas stays in Vegas!

30 **Write a book. Hurrah!** This goal is now achieved and I'm so thrilled that you've read it.

28 **Step inside the Houses of Parliament.** I'd always dreamed of visiting, and with all the work that Mum and I do as fostering ambassadors with the Department for Education, I hoped I would one day get to. In September 2016, my dream came true, but not in the way I'd envisioned – I actually attended a fashion show for the designer Zeynep Kartal. Security was tight so I couldn't take any snaps, but the building blew away my expectations.

LYDIA'S
LAST
WORD

My Nanny Maureen has a saying: 'It's not where you're from, it's where you're going,' and I guess part of that is true. I certainly believe that we can achieve anything in life no matter where we started. It's all down to hunger. Are you hungry enough to make your dreams happen?

But I'd certainly never be where I am now without where I've come from – my parents. And Essex. Life starts as a lottery. You can't help which family you get and I will forever feel blessed to have been born to Debra Jane Douglas and David Peter Bright. They taught me gratitude, to treat others how I would like to be treated, to live my dreams, and to grab every opportunity that life offers.

Writing this book has been one hell of an incredible journey. Reliving my magical childhood – being part of a crazy, chaotic, completely unique and full-of-love family – has been a joy. I learned from a young age, as one piece of a big foster-family jigsaw, that so many children are neglected, unappreciated and unloved. But these lost children came into our family home and overcame demons, disabilities and hardship to flourish into happy souls – proof that nothing is impossible with a little love.

I count my lucky stars that I am part of a massive family. I have never met a sibling group as fiercely loyal and tight as us Brights. Some of my best childhood memories are also with my grandparents, Nanny Maureen and Grandad Lou. My grandad will always be at the heart of our family and I wish he was here today to see what has happened to me. He would love the drama and excitement of it all!

Then there's *TOWIE*. My second family, which opened doors for me into the 'pinch me, is this for real?' showbiz world, and a fabulous career that enabled me to launch a business at the age of 20. Yep, Lord Sugar would be proud! I hope that my story inspires all you budding entrepreneurs to one day take the plunge into business. It sure is hard but nothing is more rewarding than building something so fruitful yourself. Gosh, I made a lot of mistakes at the beginning of *TOWIE* and when I opened Bella Sorella, but you know what they say: there's nothing like learning on the job.

The same can be said about life, I suppose. Especially relationships, which have been such a huge part of my *TOWIE* experience – the ups and downs, the trials and tribulations . . . thanks to everyone for bearing with me! Love can be the explanation for that beaming smile but also for those bright red, tear-filled eyes. Love isn't perfect. However, never forget that although a broken heart might feel like the end of the world, it's just the end of a chapter with one person. Love will continue and your world will continue spinning. Trust me.

Whether you're in a quandary about a relationship, a friendship, your education, your career or anything important to you, don't forget to follow your heart. Everyone around you will have an opinion about your best next move. The key, though, is to trust your instinct. So, when love isn't working and you feel deep inside that it's over, don't waste time trying to revive it just because your best friend says you should. Think about the long-term implications. But don't waste time regretting either – things always come good in the end. I wouldn't go back and do anything differently, even going to university. I guess travelling was my university. It educated me, enhanced me and helped me grow. Sometimes as I relived the stories of the escapades you've read within these pages I had to pinch myself. Was that really me?!

During my second trip to Cambodia I met a lady called Irene who was in her 60s and was travelling solo around the world, and I admired her courage. 'You should never limit yourself because of your age,' she told me one afternoon, and I mentally high-fived her. I hope that I'm still as exploratory, bold and brave as Irene 40 years down the line. I have been hugely lucky in life but I also believe that the harder I work the luckier I get.

We are all products of what we feel, see and do, and I hope that you've all gained a little something from the feelings and experiences I've shared with you in this book.

Grab the future with both hands, peeps – and remember . . . live, laugh and love.

Always,

Lydia x

ACKNOWLEDGMENTS

There are so many people to thank for making this dream a reality. All the people that invested so many man hours into the making of the book.

My wonderful management at Insanity Group and in particular my three fairy godmothers, Kirsty Williams, Lauren Shergold and Courtneay Yeates. Kirsty thank you for nourishing my career in every way. From the very beginning you always dreamed bigger than I ever did and so much of my success I owe to you. Lauren, you invest so much time in making sure everything is in order and without your organisation my life would be a lot more stressful, that's for sure. Courtneay – the newest member of the team – we have achieved so much in so little time and I'm so grateful for your enthusiasm.

The wonderful team on the photo shoot: Pete Pedonomou, Declan McKenna, Annie Swain, Sophie Kirkwood, Leigh Williams, Iona Blackshaw and Helen Ewing. Thanks for making the shots insane.

The people of the book world at Orion Spring, Smith and Gilmour and Bell Lomax: Gemma Calvert, Emily Barrett, Amanda Harris, Lauren Gardner, Elaine Egan, Emma Smith and Anna Bowen. You all shared my visions of this mammoth project and made it come to life, better than I ever expected it could.

Lyndsey Harrison, my makeup artist/hair stylist, and Dr Zoe Williams, my fitness guru, for contributing your incredible knowledge to these chapters.

Then I need to thank all the people that have walked into my life and made the content of the book. The TOWIE crew at Lime Pictures. Because let's be honest if it wasn't for you, I would probably be working a dead end job and nobody would want to read about that.

Then my TOWIE best friends –
I'm so glad I have experienced this
crazy world with each and every one
of you. Jessica Wright, Ferne McCann,
Lucy Meck, Georgia Kousoulou, Chloe
Lewis, Amber Dowding, Katie Wright,
James Argent, Liam Blackwell and
Tommy Mallett.

My pandas, travelling partners and
all you best friends that I have shared
treasured memories with. I pondered
on a chapter about friendship then
soon decided it would be way too
dangerous to document our
escapades. I love you more than
words can explain – Georgia Bright, Aruna MacCleay,
Danielle Park, Loren Purdy, Charlotte Pugh, Hayley Charles,
Katie Corcoran, Gabi Stein, Anna Balasuriya, Mel Tippy,
Cheryl Dabin and Laura Reid.

My family – I can never repay the support you have all given
me over the years, my biggest fans always. The love you shower
me with is unconditional and I will always count myself the
luckiest girl in the world for being part of our unit. The Brights,
Johnstons, Wiggins/Kileys, Doodys and Blacks.

And lastly, I would like to thank all of you – my audience – who
have supported me throughout the years. I will eternally be
grateful. None of this would be possible without you.

Every end is a new beginning